THE WAY PEOPLE LIVE

Life in a Wild West Show

Titles in The Way People Live series include:

Cowboys in the Old West
Life Among the Great Plains Indians
Life Among the Ibo Women of Nigeria
Life Among the Indian Fighters
Life Among the Pirates
Life Among the Samurai
Life Among the Vikings
Life During the Crusades
Life During the French Revolution
Life During the Gold Rush
Life During the Great Depression
Life During the Middle Ages
Life During the Renaissance
Life During the Russian Revolution
Life During the Spanish Inquisition
Life in a Japanese American Internment Camp
Life in Ancient Greece
Life in Ancient Rome
Life in an Eskimo Village
Life in a Wild West Show
Life in Charles Dickens's England
Life in the American Colonies
Life in the Elizabethan Theater
Life in the North During the Civil War
Life in the South During the Civil War
Life in the Warsaw Ghetto
Life in Victorian England
Life in War-Torn Bosnia
Life of a Roman Slave
Life on a Medieval Pilgrimage
Life on an Israeli Kibbutz
Life on the American Frontier

THE WAY PEOPLE LIVE

Life in a Wild West Show

by Stephen Currie

Lucent Books, P.O. Box 289011, San Diego, CA 92198-9011

Library of Congress Cataloging-in-Publication Data

Currie, Stephen, 1960–
    Life in a wild west show   / by Stephen Currie.
      p.   cm. — (The way people live)
    Includes bibliographical references (p.   ) and index.
    Summary: Discusses life in a Wild West show, including its origins, the
show content, the performers, its relation to Native Americans, moving the
show, daily life, and the death of the Wild West.
    ISBN   1-56006–352–1 (lib. : alk. paper)
    1. Wild west shows—United States—History—Juvenile literature.
[1. Wild west shows.   2. Frontier and pioneer life—West (U.S.)
3. West (U.S.)—Social life and customs.] I. Title. II. Series.
GV1833.C87   1999
791.8'4'0973—dc21   98-27233
                                              CIP
                                              AC

Contents

Discovering the Humanity in Us All

Books in The Way People Live series focus on groups of people in a wide variety of circumstances, settings, and time periods. Some books focus on different cultural groups, others, on people in a particular historical time period, while others cover people involved in a specific event. Each book emphasizes the daily routines, personal and historical struggles, and achievements of people from all walks of life.

To really understand any culture, it is necessary to strip the mind of the common notions we hold about groups of people. These stereotypes are the archenemies of learning. It does not even matter whether the stereotypes are positive or negative; they are confining and tight. Removing them is a challenge that's not easily met, as anyone who has ever tried it will admit. Ideas that do not fit into the templates we create are unwelcome visitors—ones we would prefer remain quietly in a corner or forgotten room.

The cowboy of the Old West is a good example of such confining roles. The cowboy was courageous, yet soft-spoken. His time (it is always a he, in our template) was spent alternatively saving a rancher's daughter from certain death on a runaway stagecoach, or shooting it out with rustlers. At times, of course, he was likely to get a little crazy in town after a trail drive, but for the most part, he was the epitome of inner strength. It is disconcerting to find out that the cowboy is human, even a bit childish. Can it really be true that cowboys would line up to help the

cook on the trail drive grind coffee, just hoping he would give them a little stick of peppermint candy that came with the coffee shipment? The idea of tough cowboys vying with one another to help "Coosie" (as they called their cooks) for a bit of candy seems silly and out of place.

So is the vision of Eskimos playing video games and watching MTV, living in prefab housing in the Arctic. It just does not fit with what "Eskimo" means. We are far more comfortable with snow igloos and whale blubber, harpoons and kayaks.

Although the cultures dealt with in Lucent's The Way People Live series are often historically and socially well known, the emphasis is on the personal aspects of life. Groups of people, while unquestionably affected by their politics and their governmental structures, are more than those institutions. How do people in a particular time and place educate their children? What do they eat? And how do they build their houses? What kinds of work do they do? What kinds of games do they enjoy? The answers to these questions bring these cultures to life. People's lives are revealed in the particulars and only by knowing the particulars can we understand these cultures' will to survive and their moments of weakness and greatness.

This is not to say that understanding politics does not help to understand a culture. There is no question that the Warsaw ghetto, for example, was a culture that was brought about by the politics and social ideas of Adolf

Hitler and the Third Reich. But the Jews who were crowded together in the ghetto cannot be understood by the Reich's politics. Their life was a day-to-day battle for existence, and the creativity and methods they used to prolong their lives is a vital story of human perseverance that would be denied by focusing only on the institutions of Hitler's Germany. Knowing that children as young as five or six outwitted Nazi guards on a daily basis, that Jewish policemen helped the Germans control the ghetto, that children attended secret schools in the ghetto and even earned diplomas—these are the things that reveal the fabric of life, that can inspire, intrigue, and amaze.

Books in The Way People Live series allow both the casual reader and the student to see humans as victims, heroes, and onlookers. And although humans act in ways that can fill us with feelings of sorrow and revulsion, it is important to remember that "hero," "predator," and "victim" are dangerous terms. Heaping undue pity or praise on people reduces them to objects, and strips them of their humanity.

Seeing the Jews of Warsaw only as victims is to deny their humanity. Seeing them only as they appear in surviving photos, staring at the camera with infinite sadness, is limiting, both to them and to those who want to understand them. To an object of pity, the only appropriate response becomes "Those poor creatures!" and that reduces both the quality of their struggle and the depth of their despair. No one is served by such two-dimensional views of people and their cultures.

With this in mind, The Way People Live series strives to flesh out the traditional, two-dimensional views of people in various cultures and historical circumstances. Using a wide variety of primary quotations—the words not only of the politicians and government leaders, but of the real people whose lives are being examined—each book in the series attempts to show an honest and complete picture of a culture removed from our own by time or space.

By examining cultures in this way, the reader will notice not only the glaring differences from his or her own culture, but also will be struck by the similarities. For indeed, people share common needs—warmth, good company, stability, and affirmation from others. Ultimately, seeing how people really live, or have lived, can only enrich our understanding of ourselves.

The "Real" West

The battle was short, but decisive. The several dozen cavalrymen, each dressed in standard U.S. Army gear and carrying appropriate weapons, were soon surrounded by a sea of Sioux Indians. The sound of gunshots pierced the night. Horses whinnied in alarm. The air filled with dust and blue smoke from the firearms. One by one, men slid off their mounts, fatally injured. Some were Indians, but most were white soldiers. Before long there were only a few U.S. cavalrymen left. The Sioux closed in, yelling and whooping, to finish them off. The last to die was the general, George Armstrong Custer, easily identifiable by his uniform and his long yellow hair.

The scene quieted. The Indians wheeled their horses around and rode away. The dust cleared, revealing unmoving bodies where the men had fallen. The smoke drifted away. There was silence.

Then another white man rode up. Like Custer, he was easy to recognize by the brim of his wide hat and his characteristic white goatee. William "Buffalo Bill" Cody picked his way through the fallen bodies. He paused when he came to Custer's. Taking off his hat, he held it against his chest with a mournful expression as words appeared on the huge screen behind him: "TOO LATE!"

Words on the screen? Yes. The description above was not of the actual Battle of Little Bighorn, in which Custer and all his men were killed. Instead, it described the battle as reenacted by Buffalo Bill Cody's Wild West show. Far from taking place on the plains of the West, this drama was played out in open-air arenas across the United States and Europe. The roles of Indians were indeed taken by Native Americans, though not generally those who had been in the actual battle. The

Actors reenact a battle between U.S. cavalry and American Indians in Buffalo Bill's Wild West show.

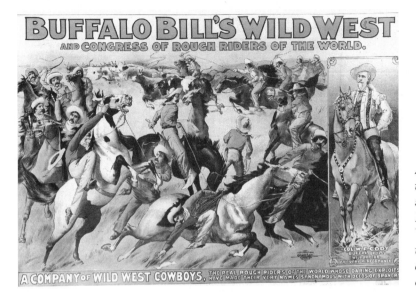

A poster from 1899 advertises Buffalo Bill's Wild West show and Congress of Rough Riders of the World. Wild West shows reenacted battles, featured trick shooting and riding, and offered other entertainment.

parts of cavalrymen, however, were taken by cowboys and other actors. The guns shot blanks, the horses were trained not to panic in the confusion, and the whole drama had been carefully scripted.

"Custer's Last Charge," as Cody called this piece, was only one of a number of dramatizations presented to audiences by his and other Wild West shows. Known for their more or less realistic demonstrations of the West and Western customs, Wild West shows were extremely popular for over thirty years. From their beginnings in 1883 all the way up to the First World War, they were everywhere, vying with each other to present the most dramatic, the most accurate, or the most exciting portrayal of the *real* West. Even today some Wild West shows continue to perform, though not in the same way as the original outfits of the turn of the century and before.

But the Wild West show was not all about excitement, drama, and adventure. Performers came from all sorts of backgrounds. Some were white Americans, others Indians, still others foreigners. Some had theatrical experience; more did not. Wild West performers and crew members put up with terrible weather, low pay, controversy, and boredom. They endured sleepless nights on cramped trains and ships. They dealt with a grueling schedule of two shows and a parade each day. Too often, the work was dangerous.

Yet many performers loved the experience. To them, the trouble was worth it. There were rewards in being part of Cody's "Wild West and Congress of Rough Riders of the World," or of "The 101 Ranch Real Wild West," or indeed of any of the countless small shows that came and went with remarkable speed. Some cast members thrived on the travel and the attention. Others were delighted to show off their skills and relive the lifestyle they knew best. And still others enjoyed being part of a truly original American entertainment. Authentic and staged; stirring and dull; exhausting and exciting: the Wild West show was all of these and more. There has been nothing quite like it, either before or since.

The Origins of the Wild West

The "Wild West." To Americans today, the image conjures up John Wayne movies, cowboy hats, photos of Indian warriors in full battle regalia. The phrase evokes saloons and frontier streets of Dodge City and Tombstone, bloody gun battles between cowboys and cattle rustlers, and lone horsemen urging their mounts across the deserts and plains.

These are the images of the West to Americans at the very end of the twentieth century, when the actual Wild West is a distant memory. But they were also the images of the West that appealed to Americans at the end of the nineteenth century, when the Wild West was still very much alive. They are the images around which the Wild West show was built. To understand the Wild West show, it is necessary to know something about the history of the American West itself.

The settling of the West by whites was a long and complicated process. Early in the nineteenth century, Thomas Jefferson sent Meriwether Lewis and William Clark to map and survey the western interior of North

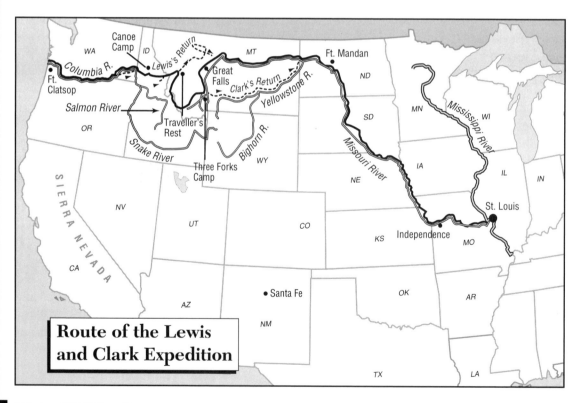

Route of the Lewis and Clark Expedition

Explorers Lewis and Clark hold a meeting with local Native Americans. Wild West shows tried to evoke the era when the West was yet to be settled and Native Americans were a real threat to westward expansion.

America. Lewis and Clark's detailed notes and records helped start a trickle of Europeans moving westward. At first these consisted mainly of trappers, traders, and soldiers, but as time went on, people began to move west to farm and establish towns as well. By 1850, Iowa, Texas, and Arkansas had all been admitted to the Union as states, and people were pushing farther west still—to the Plains and to the Rockies.

There were several obstacles to settlement of these areas. Weather was one. East of the mountains, water was scarce and farming was difficult. The northern plains and the mountains were vulnerable to blizzards and cold during the winter, while Texas and the desert regions suffered extreme heat during the summertime. Roads were poor, far worse than in the more built-up East, and distances were great. Early settlers often wrote of their terrible loneliness in diaries and letters, and many gave up frontier life after a few years and returned to the East.

The Native American Wars

But perhaps the greatest obstacle to settlement was the Indians. Many whites hated and feared the natives of the West. According to

most white soldiers and settlers, Indians were brutal uncivilized savages. For their part, many Indians resented the encroachment of the new settlers on tribal lands; they, in turn, believed that the whites were vicious and untrustworthy. This tension was nothing new; Europeans and natives had been at odds almost since the first settlement of the New World. History is full of atrocities on both sides. However, the numbers and the weapons were on the side of the whites.

Throughout the nineteenth century, the U.S. government waged a constant war against various Indian tribes. U.S. soldiers attempted, as a matter of policy, to drive Indians off their lands if those lands were wanted by whites for ranching, farming, or prospecting. Some native peoples gave up peacefully and were removed to new lands, generally barren and unwanted areas of Montana, Oklahoma, or the Dakotas. In a few cases, of course, whites soon discovered that they wanted those lands as well, and the pattern of removal began again.

Other tribes were not so quick to give in. Many Plains tribes, in particular, fought for their rights and their lands. They burned down forts, ambushed travelers and settlers, and put their hunting skills to work tracking and killing American soldiers. The army, in

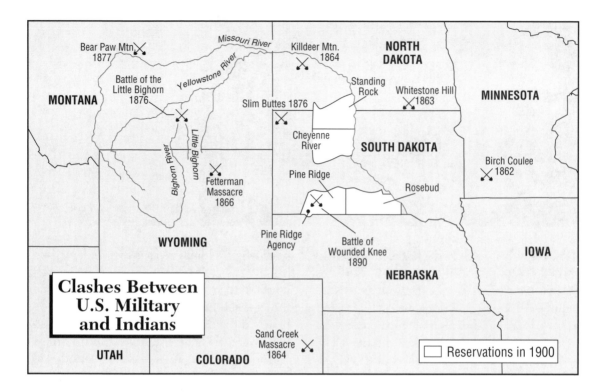

Clashes Between U.S. Military and Indians

turn, destroyed entire villages, massacred men, women, and children, and tracked stragglers through the winter snows. The army had help, too: diseases and alcohol brought, intentionally or not, by the whites, ravaged many Indian tribes. By 1890 the wars were virtually over.

The Indian wars are seen today as a blot on American national history. At the time, however, white residents of the settled, urban East and Midwest typically applauded the removal of the "wild savages" from the lands of the West. Events such as Custer's Last Stand captured the interest of Easterners who were at once attracted and repelled by the bloody stories and the artists' renditions of the battles. Danger was intriguing—especially if the reader himself was not in any danger from Indians.

But there was also a fascination with the Indians themselves. In the popular mind, In-

dians were considered as savages, unfair fighters who scalped and sneaked up on their unsuspecting civilian prey. Still, to many, Indians were intriguing. Their way of life was a curiosity, their skills and social organization obviously different from white Americans'. Their outlook was proud, almost noble. It was easy for white Americans, especially those in more settled areas of the country, to romanticize Native Americans as "noble savages," and many did.

Cowboys, Trappers, and Mountain Men

American Indians were only one part of the romantic ideal of the West. The first white men in the Plains and Rockies, for the most part, had turned their back on polite society. They headed west instead, to eke out a living in the deserts and mountains. Some were trappers, others cowboys, still others frontier scouts. They slept in the open, or they rigged shelters out of logs, brush, or whatever was available. They drifted from place to place throughout the West, never staying in one area for long unless they had to. Common to all these men, however, were two things: a horse and a gun.

Horses were not native to the American continent. Brought by early Spanish expeditions, some horses escaped and made their way to the Plains, where they found the climate and terrain to their liking. Many Plains Indian tribes captured and tamed them to make hunting buffalo easier and more efficient. American soldiers typically had horses, too, and so did the cowboys. Just as Easterners associated the West with the Indians, they also associated the West with the horse. And along with the image of the horse went the image of riders urging their mounts along mile after mile of dusty trail, pursuing Indians or tracking down stray cattle. Horsemen of the West were seen during the 1870s as brave and daring men, able to do amazing things in the course of their job that the general population could only dream of doing.

And there were guns. The popular picture of the Wild West owes much to the prevalence of guns. It was common for Westerners to carry weapons. Even with the Indians tamed, the West was a new and uneasy society in which it was never clear who was friend and who was enemy. Moreover, many Westerners relied on hunting to bring in much of their food. In the Eastern mind, the West was a place where gunfights were constantly breaking out, where men were shot for a dirty look or a poorly chosen word, where saloons were filled with gunsmoke and sound of pistol shots. In fact, the violence of the West has been overstated. Fewer cowboys, prospectors, and early settlers died in gunfire than was commonly supposed. Once again, however, the image of guns—and of people who not only knew how to use them but needed to use them as well—became a major piece of the romanticized picture of the West in the eyes of many Easterners. Along with Indians, cowboys, and horses, guns would be a central theme of Wild West shows.

Pioneers in covered wagons move across the western United States in search of a new home. The travails of such journeys were romanticized in the Wild West shows.

The Origins of the Wild West

The roots of Wild West shows lie in several types of entertainment. Perhaps the most obvious influence was the rodeo. Beginning as early as the 1840s, various Western communities had held contests at which cowboys competed to see who could do the fanciest roping and riding tricks. Early rodeos gave competitors a chance to show off their skills. Cowboys tried to stay on bucking horses as long as possible; they also lassoed cows from horseback and demonstrated unusual riding positions. "This round-up is a great time for the cowhands," a writer observed after visiting a New Mexico rodeo in 1847. "They contest with each other for the best roping and throwing, and there are horse races and whiskey and wines."[1] Some early rodeos included other acts as well. The 1876 Colorado State Fair, for instance, featured a race between a cowboy and a horse. Many rodeo acts, changed slightly, became part of Wild West shows.

The tradition of the circus also contributed to the development of the Wild West show. Traveling circuses were quite common, though not always well respected, in nineteenth century America. Many moved from one town to the next, giving a performance or two and then heading out again, in a pattern to be repeated by the Wild West shows later in the century. Moreover, many of these circuses had small menageries, consisting perhaps of a bear, a mountain lion, and a mangy dog passed off as a wolf. A few early menageries had Western themes. One menagerie owner, James Adams, was known as "Grizzly"; not only did he have three grizzly bears as part of his show, but he liked to ride on the back of the largest one during his circus parades. Animals—horses, elk, and buffalo in particular—would become central parts of the Wild West show as well.

And occasionally the Western tourism industry took on Wild West aspects. It was common for wealthy Easterners and Europeans to hire guides to take them in search of big game. These trips were often serious, but some were more focused on entertainment. During the 1870s, for instance, an entrepreneur named Joseph McCoy advertised a Western hunting trip as a "Grand Excursion

(Left) A cowboy rides a bucking bronco. (Right) An Indian uses his horse to avoid fire from nearby covered wagons. Wild West shows hired men to perform such stunts as entertainment.

A traveling circus goes through the center of Salida, Colorado, in the early 1900s. Wild West shows were part traveling circus, part rodeo.

to the Far West! A Wild and Exciting Chase after the Buffalo, on his Native Plain." McCoy provided horses and camping equipment, but told participants to "bring their own firearms."[2] Shooting buffalo was part of the point, but the title made it clear that McCoy was also selling the Western experience.

Finally, there were stage melodramas and dime novels. Melodramas had been around for many years before the first Wild West show appeared. They were plays with no pretension to literary merit. Typically they were put on by touring companies and featured easily identifiable heroes, villains, and damsels in distress. Audiences participated by hissing and booing the villains and applauding the hero and heroine. By the 1870s, Western themes were very common in touring melodramas. One historian writes,

> The forces of good were pitted against the forces of evil in suitable Western settings. The heroes were plainsmen or hunters, the villains Indians, bandits, or Mexicans. . . . Often the heroes' roles were played by those who had actually been there. . . . The villains were played by stock actors, and the obligatory Indians by people hired off the street. The audience was always treated to much gunfire

and spectacle (prairie fires, cyclones, and floods were not unknown), and a horse almost always made an appearance somewhere in the course of the evening.[3]

Easterners not only loved to watch this type of dramatic performance, they also liked to read about the West. By 1870 a whole genre of literature had sprung up to fill this need: the Western novel. Called "dime novels" because they were cheap to sell and produce, these Westerns sold thousands and thousands of copies. Like melodramas, dime novels were usually exciting, but not particularly authentic. They dealt with the settings and situations of the West as Eastern audiences imagined it to be, complete with stagecoach robberies, knife fights, and marauding Indians. Dime novels were popular in Europe as well: one German author, Karl May, wrote thirty-five enormously successful Westerns despite never having been to America.

Buffalo Bill

In the early 1880s, melodramas, dime novels, traveling circuses, rodeos, and Western hunting trips all came together into a true Wild West show. The man who did it was a famous

Melodrama

Utterly predictable and always sentimental, melodramas were written on extremely tight schedules, then cast and produced on schedules tighter still. Buffalo Bill was shocked to discover what the timetables actually were. In his autobiography, *Story of the Wild West and Camp-Fire Chats*, Cody relates a discussion between Ned Buntline, author of *The Scouts of the Plains*, and a man named Nixon, who owned the theater in which the play was to be presented.

"'I am ready for you, Buntline. Have you got your company yet?' asked Nixon.

'No, sir; but there are plenty of idle theatrical people in town, and I can raise a company in two hours,' was his reply.

'You haven't much time to spare, if you open on Monday night,' said Nixon. 'If you will allow me to look at your drama, to see what kind of people you want, I'll assist you in organizing your company.'

'I have not yet written the drama,' said Buntline.

'What the deuce do you mean? This is Wednesday, and you propose to open on next Monday night. The idea is ridiculous. Here you are at this late hour without a company and without a drama.'"

Buntline did not share Nixon's concerns. He wrote the play in one four-hour sitting and found his actors that same afternoon. The play was not well reviewed, but that was a common fate of melodramas. Cody was especially fond of quoting the review in the Chicago *Inter-Ocean*. Buntline, playing a character named Cale Durg, was killed off in the second act. The *Inter-Ocean* reviewer commented that it was a shame Buntline's character had not been killed during the first!

---

name in Western history: William F. Cody, better known as "Buffalo Bill." Born in Iowa on February 26, 1846, Cody spent time as a frontier scout, a cowboy, and a buffalo hunter, among several other occupations, before turning to show business around 1872. At first Cody performed in Western melodramas. His name was already well known to Eastern audiences, partly through the success of some dime novels that featured him as the main character. Cody's first play was entitled *The Scouts of the Prairie*. Others were called *The Knight of the Plains* and *Buffalo Bill, the King of Border Men*. Cody always considered himself a bad actor, and most critics agreed. Nevertheless, he liked touring the country as a stage performer. While Cody typically did not write his own material, he had a hand in plan-

ning the performances, and the name of his troupe—the "Buffalo Bill Combination"—reflects his influence.

Settling into a life of show business was hard for Cody. He found learning lines almost impossible: after seeing the script for *The Scouts of the Prairie*, he estimated that it would take about six months to memorize the part. "I thought it was the hardest work I had ever done,"[4] he remembered years later. Indeed, he forgot all his lines on stage during the first performance of the play. Instead, he improvised, telling a story of a buffalo hunt. "In this way," he recalled later, "I took up fifteen minutes, without once speaking a word of my part; nor did I speak a word of it the whole evening." The audience loved it, however. Cody congratulated himself on making "such a brilliant and successful debut," and added years later, "There was no backing out after that."[5]

Like competing melodramas, Cody's earliest plays included many elements of what were to become Wild West shows. A program from one performance mentions scenes such as "The Scalp Dance," "The Knife Fight," and "The Prairie on Fire."[6] Forty or fifty extras were hired to play the parts of Indians, and Cody and his co-star, a frontier scout named Texas Jack, thoroughly enjoyed the reenactment of the Indian wars. Cody wrote in an autobiography:

The cover of a dime novel romanticizes the exploits of Buffalo Bill. William Cody originally became well known to people in the East through the circulation of such novels.

Jack and I were at home. We blazed away at each other with blank cartridges; and when the scene ended in a hand-to-hand encounter—a general knock-down and drag-out—the way Jack and I killed Indians was "a caution" [amazing]. We would kill them all off in one act, but they would come up again ready for business in the next.[7]

Although critics commonly panned the acting and the plot, they were much more enthusiastic about the Wild West elements. A Boston newspaper, for instance, called *The Scouts of the Prairie* "an extraordinary production with more wild Indians, scalping knives and gun powder to the square inch than any drama ever before heard of."[8] Where these features were played down or eliminated, however, people's reactions were quite different. "The small boy and the lover of western romance were disappointed," wrote another reviewer in 1879. "There were no buffalo, no black bears, no wild Indians; but instead a third-rate dramatic company, playing at some sort of sickly play without point or pith."[9]

"A Noisy, Rattling, Gunpowder Entertainment"

Cody was a quick study. Before long he realized that the Western pageantry was what audiences had come to see. Accordingly, he began to move away from the stock conventions of melodrama plots and toward more and more Western elements in his shows. By 1880, Cody had introduced sharpshooting into his plays. The drama *The Prairie Waif* included a demonstration of riflery starring Cody himself, and the advertising emphasized this aspect of the show. "The audience will please take particular notice of the twenty different positions that Mr. Cody holds his rifle in making the fancy shots,"[10] read one newspaper review of the play.

Cody's casting of Indians also spoke to this change and to Cody's desire for realism. In the original productions of *The Scouts of the Prairie* all Native American roles were played by non-Indian actors from Chicago, in typical Western melodrama style. Before long, however, these white men were replaced by actual Indians, including several chiefs of the Pawnee nation. Cody could have hired white actors without most people knowing the difference, but he wanted the shows to be as accurate as possible.

As for the plays themselves, Cody soon saw them as vehicles for shooting, fighting, and Western costumes. "It made no difference at which act we commenced the performance," Cody said about one five-act play he had commissioned. "It afforded us, however, ample opportunity to give a noisy, rattling, gunpowder entertainment, and to present a succession of scenes in the late Indian war."[11] According to one biographer, in the decade between his first melodrama and his last one, Cody had come a long way:

> He learned that it was not fine acting, in the accepted meaning of the phrase, that was most popular with the people. It was the appearance of real Indians, real guides, real scouts, real cowboys, real buffaloes, real bucking horses, and last but not least, real Buffalo Bill, who had already become in the minds of the American people the Ideal American Plainsman.[12]

The "Old Glory Blow Out"

In 1882, Cody returned to his home in North Platte, Nebraska, after a theatrical tour. He was immediately put in charge of organizing an Independence Day celebration. Cody made the most of the opportunity. Early in 1882, Cody had met with an actor and theater manager named Nate Salsbury, and the two men had discussed vague plans for a traveling exhibition that would feature buffaloes, cowboys, Indians, and horses. The Independence Day celebration, Cody realized, was an excellent chance to try out some of these ideas.

Cody's plans for what he called the "Old Glory Blow Out" were large and became larger as the date for the celebration approached. Certainly, the festival was one of the biggest rodeos held to that point. Cody spared no expense to make this rodeo the best ever. He got townspeople to donate prizes for

Texas Jack was a performer in Buffalo Bill's melodrama troop. Cody aimed for accuracy in his shows, including hiring Native Americans and real cowboys.

P. T. Barnum and the Wild West

Although Buffalo Bill was the first to put together a true Wild West show, the great showman Phineas T. Barnum occasionally used Western themes in his exhibitions. In 1843, for instance, Barnum staged a "Grand Buffalo Hunt" in Hoboken, New Jersey. Barnum promised a thrilling afternoon of watching cowboys lasso and chase a herd of dangerous buffaloes. People flocked to the show, especially from New York City across the Hudson River.

The show was one of Barnum's famous hoaxes, however. The buffaloes were old and weak. As Neil Harris writes in his book *Humbug: The Art of P. T. Barnum*, they were "hardly capable of movement, much less of violence." In the end they ran off and hid in a swamp. Barnum charged no admission but made money from the "show" anyway. He had made a deal with ferryboat operators to take a percentage of their profits for bringing passengers across the Hudson that day.

The next month, Barnum hired some Native Americans for an exhibit in his American Museum in New York City. The Indians were billed as bloodthirsty savages, and Barnum played this angle up: he had them perform war dances in full costume. The dances were so realistic they occasionally made spectators fear for their lives. In private, however, Barnum complained that the Indians lacked energy. "The lazy devils want to be lying down nearly all the time," he wrote a colleague, "and as it looks so bad for them to be lying about the Museum, I have them stretched out in the work shop all day." Like the Great Buffalo Hunt, Barnum's Indian exhibition was profitable, though. Barnum planned to expand both these ventures into exhibitions similar to Cody's first Wild West shows, but never did much with Western themes during his long and brilliant career."

the best ropers, riders, and bronco busters. He sent out advertisements looking for competitors and expected one hundred cowboys to enter; instead, he got about a thousand.

The festival included a demonstration of a buffalo hunt as well. Cody and a few friends chased buffalo around the town's racetrack, firing blanks from horseback. The demonstration was to be entertaining as well as educational. Still, rodeos and buffalo hunts had been done before, even if not on the same scale as in North Platte. What set Cody's show apart was the quality and depth of the festival. Cody hired Native Americans and cowboys to wander the grounds and give the celebration a uniquely Western flavor. Cowhands gave marksmanship demonstrations. Old friends of Cody's staged horse races. Indians and trap-

pers wore typical Western clothing and acted out aspects of frontier life. As in a modern-day county fair, there was always something happening at this Independence Day celebration, and as often as not, the "something" involved the Wild West.

The First Wild West Show

The Old Glory Blow Out was a huge success. One exaggerated account insisted that "the whole country for a radius of one hundred and fifty miles" was "temporarily depopulated."[13] Whatever the true attendance figures, Cody knew he had a winner on his hands. According to a North Platte resident, Cody began that day to plan an outdoor

To raise money for his Wild West show, William Cody turned to two men: Nate Salsbury (left), a theater manager and actor, and William Carver (right), a sharpshooter.

traveling Wild West show based on his melodramas and the North Platte festival.

That fall Cody returned to the Buffalo Bill Combination. He was already at work organizing his summer exhibition, however. For this he became partners with another plainsman, a sharpshooter named William Frank "Doc" Carver. Carver's main contribution was money; he put up nearly thirty thousand dollars to help open the show. Cody then asked Salsbury to join the venture as well. Salsbury, however, had wanted to wait until 1884 to try to mount a show. Moreover, he was not pleased to discover that Cody had joined forces with Carver. "I was dumfounded," Salsbury recalled afterwards, "and replied that I did not want to have anything to do with Doctor Carver."[14] As far as Salsbury was concerned, Carver was a slippery character who knew a lot less about the West than he claimed. Salsbury wished Cody the best of luck, but predicted failure for his new venture.

He was half right. Cody was well prepared for planning Wild West acts, but not good at the financial and organizational pieces of running a company. The show, named "The Wild West, Hon. W. F. Cody and Dr. W. F. Carver's Rocky Mountain and Prairie Exhibition," opened in Omaha on May 17, 1883. After that, it toured the Midwest and New England for several months, before settling into a five-week run at Coney Island, New York. The show returned to Nebraska after crisscrossing the Midwest again, closing in Omaha late in the fall.

The Program

Cody chose his program well. Twelve acts comprised the typical show. Beginning with a Grand Introductory March, the program included horse races, shooting exhibitions, roping and riding events, and two dramas. One was an attack on a mail coach. The other was a gun battle between soldiers and Indians, which closed the show.

These acts required a huge cast and many props and stage sets. Cody took his time getting the right actors and materials. He placed a heavy value on authenticity and education; while a program was supposed to entertain, Cody always wanted his audiences to learn something as well. Consequently, Cody hired as many actual Westerners as he could. "After several months of patient work," Cody wrote in an autobiography, "I secured the services of nearly fifty cow-boys and Mexicans skilled in lasso-throwing and famous as daring riders."[15] He also brought in buffalo, elk, and mountain sheep, along with seventy saddle horses, and purchased an old stagecoach that had once been attacked by Indians. The stagecoach was to be pulled by Western mules and driven by a professional stagecoach driver. To play the Indians, Cody hired thirty-six Pawnees under the direction of former army officer Frank North.

Cody's passion for authenticity was not shared by everyone, however. At an early rehearsal, the town council of Columbus, Nebraska, was invited to sit in the stagecoach while the performers practiced "Attack on the Deadwood Mail Coach." Unfortunately, the mules pulling the stagecoach were not accustomed to their job. When the Pawnees charged the coach, yelling and firing blanks, the mules panicked. No one was hurt, but tempers flew. Frank North was especially perturbed. He told Cody,

Bill, if you want to make this damned show go, you do not need me or my Indians. You want about twenty old bucks [elderly warriors who no longer fought]. Fix them up with all the paint and feathers in the market. Use some old hack horses and a hack driver. To make it go you want a show of illusion, not realism.[16]

North's advice did not deter Cody, however. The first Wild West show remained mainly authentic throughout its travels.

Separate Ways

While the show was popular, especially in the East, it proved unable to make much money. Advertising costs were high, start-up costs higher, and neither Carver nor Cody seemed able to control spending. Both partners accused each other of being drunk on the job and never pulling his share of the work. Indeed, according to several accounts, Carver was too drunk to perform his sharpshooting act for some of the show's early performances. His position was taken by Cody, which led to professional jealousy between the two men. At the end of the season, Carver wanted to continue with a winter tour of the South; Cody refused. "Cody came to see me," Nate Salsbury reported later, "and said that if I did not take hold of the show he was going to quit the whole thing. He said he was through with Carver and that he would not go through such another summer for a hundred thousand dollars."[17]

Cody was indeed discouraged, but he could and did take pride in his first season. Together he and Carver had put together a show that people wanted to see. He had worked hard to build a realistic and exciting program. He and Carver divided up the remaining assets of the show and planned for the future. For both of them—and for many other entrepreneurs and Westerners who had been observing their success—the future was to include the Wild West.

The Shows

Doc Carver spent the winter of 1883–1884 touring the South with his show, renamed "The Carver and Crawford Wild West" after himself and his new partner, a scout named Jack Crawford. As for Buffalo Bill Cody, he joined forces with Nate Salsbury and set out again in the spring of 1884. These two shows set the standard for what was to come. Within three or four years there would be another dozen Wild West shows on the market, and the number kept growing. Historian Don Russell has identified well over a hundred different Wild West outfits and says the list is probably far from complete. Some performed only briefly and in a limited area, while others, such as Cody's, were nationally famous and went on for many years. All, however, can trace their origins back to Carver and Cody's first Wild West tour in the summer of 1883.

Of course, the various Wild West shows were different from each other in many ways. For every show like Cody's, which stressed size, pageantry, and accuracy, there were many more fly-by-night companies that promised much and offered little. Russell points out that Wild West shows were easy to fake. "Whereas even the smallest of circuses required at least one elephant, a lion or two, a band wagon, and a calliope," he writes, "a Wild West show could get by with a stagecoach and a covered wagon."[18] Nor was authenticity a goal for all companies. One Wild West show, for instance, was organized in Philadelphia. Its backers hired Philadelphia

Entertainers in the Wild West show perform an acrobatic feat. Most Wild West shows featured about twenty acts that included sharpshooting, horsemanship, and battle reenactments.

"cowboys" who could not ride, rope, or shoot. The company did not last long.

By 1890, the Wild West show pattern had been set. Cody's show was probably the most famous of all shows, but others were well known and influential as well. Adam Forepaugh, a circus owner, got into the Wild West business early on. His "Forepaugh and Wild West Combination," sometimes known as "4-Paw's Wild West," was a big success. Gordon Lillie, also known as Pawnee Bill, had been an interpreter for the Pawnee Indians on Carver and Cody's 1883 tour. In 1888, he opened his own show, "The Pawnee Bill Historical Wild West Exhibition and Indian Encampment." Years later he and Cody would merge their competing shows into one. Joe, Zack, and George Miller founded "The Miller Brothers 101 Ranch Real Wild West," which was perhaps the largest of all. Each of these companies contributed to the development of the Wild West show.

By the 1890s, a typical Wild West show included about twenty different acts. Guns, horses, Indians, and cowboys, separately or together, made up the majority of them. Existing Cody programs from the 1890s show this emphasis quite clearly. Of the nineteen acts (plus overture and conclusion) listed in the 1893 program, for instance, eight involved Native Americans and seven included cowboys or frontier scouts. There were three sharpshooting exhibitions, with most of the other acts featuring firearms in some way, and displays of horsemanship were part of virtually every act as well. Each of these pieces was vital to the production of a Wild West show.

Sharpshooting

Marksmanship, for instance, was a natural event for a show. The ability to shoot quickly and accurately was an important skill to cowboys, hunters, and soldiers alike. The Western man—or woman—who shot with deadly accuracy was admired and occasionally feared. Large shows had two or three sharpshooting acts, scattered throughout the program. Typically the shooters wore genuine Western outfits; they performed one at a time or in pairs.

Sharpshooters used shotguns or rifles. For most demonstrations the guns were loaded with fine buckshot rather than bullets. This was for safety purposes. It ensured that a stray shot would not seriously hurt any spectator or performer. One story, possibly untrue, says that Carver and Cody used real bullets in their first performance, but stopped the practice after that show when they received a bill for replacing broken windows in a greenhouse eight blocks from the arena where they were performing. Whatever the truth of the story, most Wild West sharpshooters preferred not to take a chance of damage or injury; they used shot.

Part of the sharpshooting acts demonstrated shooting accuracy. Assistants tossed marbles or clay targets in the air for the marksman to hit. The shooter would fire again and again until as many as possible had been knocked out of the air. This was a variation of a sport known as trapshooting. Audiences were usually appreciative. A boy who saw the great Annie Oakley perform at one show never forgot it:

> The band started playing and she made her entrance dressed in full western style, riding on a very nice bronco. Along side of her was an Indian riding a western pony carrying a basket of white glass balls about the size of a golf ball. Finally, they got their horses on a gallop and the Indian would throw a ball one at a time up in the air and Miss Oakley would aim and fire and never miss a ball—each one breaking in many pieces.[19]

Sharpshooters showed off their aim and steady hand in other ways too. Some performers extinguished a candle flame with a single shot, or—William Tell style—shot an apple off a dog's head. Though accuracy was the point of the demonstrations, the most popular sharpshooters occasionally missed shots on purpose. Years of experience showed them that audiences tired of watching nothing but success. Moreover, an occasional miss added to the tension when a performer was about to attempt a really hard shot.

Horses are driven over a barrier as men stand on their backs. Daredevil riding was a common feature of Wild West shows.

Finally, sharpshooting acts usually included trick shots. Accuracy was important here too, but performers added extra layers to make them harder—and more exciting. These tricks varied considerably according to the performer. Some shot while hanging upside down from a moving horse. Others showed off their quickness. Lillian Smith of Cody's troupe was proud of her ability to hit a target thirty times in fifteen seconds. The great Annie Oakley had targets thrown into the air; then she jumped across a table, picked up her rifle, and shot them down. Buffalo Bill never considered himself a "fancy shot," but impressed audiences with his ability to shoot without sighting along his gun first. After many years of practice, he had learned to aim simply by feel.

Horsemanship and Cowboys

Just as Wild West shows hired some of the best sharpshooters in the United States, so did they employ some of the most capable riders around. Nearly every Wild West show, no matter how small, had at least one former cowboy to perform riding and roping tricks, and larger Wild West shows employed dozens of horsemen. Indians, too, often performed on horseback, either with the cowboys or as part of a separate act. The most basic horsemanship demonstration was what Cody called "Cow-Boy Fun." This act included events like those of a modern-day rodeo. One program described the act as "picking objects from the ground, lassoing wild horses, riding the buckers, etc." [20]

"Cow-Boy Fun" was wildly popular. Henry Irving, an Englishman who attended a show in Chicago in 1893, remembered the excitement the cowboys stirred up. "Such daredevil riding was never seen on earth," he wrote afterward. "When the American cowboys sweep like a tornado up the track, forty or fifty strong, every man swinging his hat and every pony at its utmost speed, a roar of wonder and delight breaks from the thousands in the grandstand." [21]

Nor were all the riders men. Colonel Zack Mulhall's Wild West starred Zack's daughter Lucille. Lucille Mulhall was among the most famous of Wild West performers. She was known for her bronco busting and lassoing skills. Other women were featured, too. Pawnee Bill advertised "beautiful daring western girls and Mexican senoritas in a contest of equine skill";[22] a poster shows women riding bucking broncos, standing on horseback, and running alongside wild horses. Wild West women often demonstrated so-called "Roman" riding, in which performers linked several horses together side to side and rode standing up, with a foot on each of the outside horses. And occasionally women riders were asked to take on tasks that were quite dangerous. Doc Carver, for instance, featured a forty-foot dive into a water tank by a woman on horseback.

Not all horse demonstrations involved trick riding, however. Cody's show presented several horse-racing acts, including bareback races, a hundred-yard race between a man and a horse, and a jumping contest billed as "Hurdle Race between Primitive Riders mounted on Western Broncho Ponies."[23] Other companies featured parades of exotic horses, or showed off horses trained to respond to commands given by their riders. Emma Hickok, "The Champion Equestrienne of the World,"[24] taught her horse to

stand on its hind legs and "bow" to acknowledge applause. And a few shows had riders guiding their horses through the steps of a square dance or Virginia reel.

Indians performed as riders, of course, but they also filled another role. If the cowboys seemed exotic to Eastern audiences, then the Indians were much more so. Not only were they a different race, but their languages, customs, and appearance were quite different as well. Probably most Easterners had never seen an Indian up close. A touring Wild West show gave them a chance to see not just one, but a whole band of Indians for the first time. Show promoters made sure the crowds were not disappointed. They dressed the Indians in typical native clothing, complete with war paint and feathers. Not only did they play up the riding skills of their Indians; they also had acts in which Native Americans performed traditional songs, dances, and ceremonies. Indians were a central part of the Wild West experience. Audiences clamored to see them, and promoters generally gave the customers what they wanted.

Horsemen turn out for the "Grand Entry," the opening act of Cody's Wild West shows.

Foreign Riders

Indeed, several shows built on this foundation. Moving beyond Western cowboy and Indian skills, they set out to offer a more international flavor. Cody, for instance, brought in Mexican riders known as vaqueros. They wore genuine Mexican outfits and demonstrated lassoing and riding tricks. Cody went further afield, too, bringing in gauchos, or Argentine cowboys; Russian horsemen known as Cossacks; and various horsemen from eastern Asia, the Middle East, and Australia—the latter the idea of Cody's partner, Nate Salsbury.

Other Wild West shows also hired foreigners to broaden the range of acts available

Injuries and Dangers

"Football on horseback" and mock hangings were not the only dangerous parts of Wild West performances. Working closely with guns, buffalo, and wild horses caused many injuries—and a few deaths—to show personnel over the years. Major Frank North, who had urged Cody to replace the Pawnee Indian warriors with older, more docile men, was one of the first casualties of the Wild West show. During an 1884 performance of trick riding in Hartford, Connecticut, North was thrown by his horse and trampled by another one. It turned out that his saddle cinch, or strap, had broken. North never recovered; he died the following March.

Cody himself was seriously injured during an 1883 event he called "Lassoing and Riding the Wild Bison of the Plains." The best riders hired by Cody had succeeded in riding all the buffalo the show owned with one exception: a big bull named Monarch. Cody ordered Monarch roped and ridden during a performance in Indianapolis. His cowboys managed to rope and throw Monarch, but refused to attempt the ride. Cody climbed on, was bucked off, and spent two weeks in the hospital. It was the last time that particular event appeared in a Cody program.

Innocent bystanders were sometimes hurt as well. During one of sharpshooter Johnny Baker's acts, he accidentally fired a shot through the side wall of the arena. The shot pierced the canvas and struck "Cossack Tom" Oliver, an interpreter for the Cossacks, in both an eye and an ear. Oliver recovered, but his example shows the danger Wild West shows posed to anyone who spent time with them.

And even when performers were not seriously hurt, minor injuries were all too common. The 101 Ranch show estimated that from one to six cowboys a day needed medical attention after being thrown, kicked, or bitten. A Cody performer was cut when his horse ran too near a barbed wire fence. Another cowboy was thrown during a performance and lost his false teeth.

When the Cody show journeyed to England, injuries were especially common—and to hear Cody tell it, expected. One cowboy broke a leg shortly after the performances began. Nor was he the last. "The Englishmen got so that if nobody was hurt during a performance they were disappointed," Cody remembered, as quoted in Joseph G. Rosa and Robin May's book, *Buffalo Bill and His Wild West: A Pictorial Biography*, "so when no one was hurt, I would instruct one of the boys to pretend to be injured, and they wouldn't know the difference." It was one of the few occasions when Cody was deliberately less than authentic in his show.

Cody was one of the first to use Mexican riders known as vaqueros (left) in his shows. In a reenactment (below), a vaquero forces his horse to lie on the ground for use as cover while he shoots at an enemy.

and to show the audience a touch of the exotic. In Cody's show, however, foreign riders were so important that by 1893 he had subtitled his Wild West show "Congress of Rough Riders of the World." At various times during performances, the ethnic groups would have a chance to show off their particular skills. The Cossacks, for instance, performed traditional Russian maneuvers along with dances from their homeland; once again, the educational aspect of the performance was important to Cody. He also advertised Syrian and Arabian horsemen. According to the program, they would "illustrate their style of Horsemanship, with Native Sports and Pastimes."[25]

Though the specifics of these acts varied from performance to performance, the general outlines did not. Cody became well known for staging races between six riders of different origins, each mounted on a horse native to his own area. He also took to beginning his productions with a "Grand Entry" or "Grand Review," in which horsemen from all over the world took part. A Baltimore newspaper reported,

In intricate and amazing evolutions, the horsemen whirled and dashed back and forth, performing difficult maneuvers so rapidly that the eye could hardly follow. The cowgirls swept to the ground for their handkerchiefs while at full speed and regained their seats without apparent effort. The Indians with feathers streaming in the wind created by their own mad speed, threaded the pitching, twisting mass of horsemen with unerring eye, their shrill whoops pulsating weirdly through the crowded pavilions. Cossacks and Cingalese [Singhalese], Dahomeans [West Africans], Mexicans, South American vaqueros and American cowboys—they swayed hither and thither on caracoling [turning] horses in a magnificent flash of vivid and contrasting color.[26]

Although there was a good chance that at least some of the Dahomeans and others were not actually as billed, many audience recollections of Wild West shows focus especially on images such as this one.

Dramas

But the centerpiece of Wild West shows was Western-themed drama. Cowboys, Indians, guns, and horses all came together in these dramatizations of actual or imagined Western events. Once again, Cody was the innovator in this area. An 1894 show program, for instance, includes four separate dramas, all of them pitting cowboys, soldiers, and scouts against Indians: an attack on a covered wagon, the capture of a mail stagecoach, the famous reenactment of the Battle of Little Bighorn, and an attack on a settler's cabin, which culminated in "rescue by Buffalo Bill and a band of Cow-boys, Scouts, and Frontiersmen."[27] The pageants were excuses for plenty of shouting, riding, and gunfire, and many a children's game of cops and robbers or cowboys and Indians has been based, at least indirectly, on them.

These acts were certainly dramatic. The "Attack upon the Deadwood Stage" had volunteers from the audience riding in the stagecoach. "Should you meet with Indians," the ringmaster instructed the driver of the coach, "put on the whip, and if possible, save the lives of your passengers."[28] Everyone knew the attack would happen, but no one knew exactly when—leading to genuine screams from the audience when the moment arrived.

"Attack upon a Settler's Cabin" began with Indians sneaking up to a log cabin. When

A Native American and a Cossack pose in costume for Cody's Wild West show. Foreign riders were so important to Cody's show that he eventually subtitled it the "Congress of Rough Riders of the World."

one tried to make off with a horse, the settler's son discovered them and fired at the thief. At that point an entire band of Native Americans swooped down on the cabin, whereupon cowboys arrived with their guns blazing. "With enough firing of pistols in it to make the small boy howl with delight," reported one observer, "men shot from their saddles and riderless steeds dashing around, the cowboys won their victory and the cabin was saved."[29]

Though Cody originated the idea of these dramatic presentations, other shows soon equaled or surpassed him. Pawnee Bill presented a Great Train Robbery. Adam Forepaugh presented his own version of Custer's Last Stand. The killing of white settlers and soldiers by Indians was an especially popular topic for dramas. Several shows featured a reenactment of the Mountain Meadows Massacre of 1857. The 101 Ranch Wild West show dramatized the "Pat Hennessey

Massacre," an Indian attack on a group traveling through Oklahoma in 1875. U.S. Marshal W. H. Malaley eventually arrived at the scene, but too late to save any of the travelers. As a man who had seen the show described it,

The 101 Ranch reenacted the tragic prairie drama in all its details. To give added realism [the show owners hired] Mr. Malaley who went through his movements exactly as performed at the scene of the original massacre. Chief Bull Bear of the Cheyennes was generally accredited with being the author of the murder. He, too, was in the 101 Ranch show arena.[30]

Perhaps the most dramatic event ever staged was Pawnee Bill's version of a frontier hanging. Frank Sylvis played the horse thief who became the victim of frontier justice. Twice a day he was jerked off his horse and pulled along the ground by means of a rope.

A telegraph pole at one end of the arena is the destination. The rope is looped over the cross-piece and Sylvis, half strangled and choking with smoke and dust, is hauled high in the air. His life seems to go out with a last few spasmodic kicks, and he hangs limp until cut loose by the sheriff and the posse.[31]

Although the dramatization was only pretend, Sylvis said that his fear of actual hanging was always very real. Nevertheless, he added, "it's the best paying job with the show, and I'll stick to it till they put me out of business."[32]

Setting the Mood

The effect of these acts was heightened by several additions to help set the mood. An orator, a cross between a ringmaster and a narrator, ran the show and introduced the acts. When possible, show promoters preferred to line up genuine Westerners with box office draw for this part. When this was not possible, anyone with a loud voice who looked reasonably like a typical Westerner would do. The orator was either dressed in a suit or decked out in Western wear, complete with hat, cowboy boots, and buckskin jacket.

In this reenactment, Buffalo Bill saves a lady from savage Native Americans. Such dramatizations were a major part of the Wild West show.

Most large companies hired bands as well, which provided overtures, marches, and musical accompaniment as necessary. "It is the cowboy band," wrote one newspaper reviewer of Cody's show, "which supplies the obbligato to [helps to highlight] the bucking of the broncos, the raids of the redskins, and the antics of the Arabs."[33] Both the band and the orator helped move the show along and keep dramatic tension alive.

Props, sets, and scenery were other important ways of helping the show along. Their complexity depended partly on the acts being shown, and partly on the location of the show. Companies that often moved from one town to another could not use set pieces as extensive as shows that performed at the same site night after night. Many companies, however, had at least one or two large canvas Western-style backdrops, showing mountains, deserts, or plains, perhaps with a buffalo or two sketched in the background.

Some companies also used stagecoaches, tepees, tents, or covered wagons during the show. When possible these were authentic; when necessary they were pieced together by designers experienced in theatrical illusion. The Cody show, for instance, used a genuine stagecoach, but built a "log cabin" out of flat boards. When the company needed a train in the early twentieth century, the crew constructed a

In this photograph cast members enact the drama of a hunter returning to hearth and home while his long-suffering wife greets his arrival. Notice the mountain backdrop and simple props that make up the cabin.

"The Impromptu and the Unforeseen"

One of the great charms of the Wild West show was that it often did not go completely as planned. British actor Henry Irving was especially impressed with the ability of Cody's cast to manage uncertainties. He is quoted here in Cody's autobiography *Story of the Wild West and Camp-Fire Chats*:

"You have real cowboys, with bucking horses, real buffaloes, and great numbers of cows, which are lassoed and stampeded in the most realistic fashion imaginable. Then there are real Indians, who execute attacks upon coaches driven at full speed. . . . However well it may be rehearsed—and the greatest care is taken that it shall go properly—it is impossible to avoid a considerable share of the impromptu and the unforeseen. For you may rehearse with buffaloes as much as you like, but no one can say in what way they will stampede when they are suddenly turned loose in the open. No one can say how the ox has to be lassoed, or in what way the guns have to be fired when the border fight comes on."

scaled-down version of the outside of a train engine and placed it over an automobile. Sets and scenery, whether authentic or not, were meant to add to the Westernness of the show.

Wild West and Far East

As time went on, the focus of Wild West dramas began to change slightly. With many different Wild West companies on tour, most of them offering more or less similar acts, promoters began to look for new and exciting areas to mine. A few added elephants, lions, and other animals, thus becoming a cross between a traveling menagerie and an actual Wild West show. Alternatively, producers broadened the types of entertainments they offered. Some shows, for instance, added dramatizations of current events, such as the "Charge up San Juan Hill" from the 1898 Spanish-American War or the "Capture of Peking" from the 1900 Boxer Rebellion in China. Others went back into time, giving demonstrations of chariot races or reenacting John Smith and Pocahontas at Jamestown.

The most common additions, though, had Asian themes. When Pawnee Bill and Buffalo Bill went into business together as partners in 1909, they called the resulting production "Buffalo Bill's Wild West and Pawnee Bill's Far East Combined." Pawnee Bill brought in Australian aborigines with boomerangs, Chinese soldiers, and magicians from India. Every performance of this new show included an act called "The Far East or a Dream of the Orient." This act featured dancing elephants and other animals, along with what a 1909 program of the show called "an ethnological congress of strange tribes, clans, races, and nations of peculiar people."[34] The Miller and Arlington Wild West Show Company featured acrobats from Japan and the Middle East. Other companies followed suit.

But Wild West shows rarely moved far away from their original purpose. Even when promoters added something new, they often wove it into Western themes. One of the more unusual acts of any Wild West show was a ball game that Cody included in several of his programs. The game, called "Football on Horseback," was a favorite with audiences but was disliked intensely by performers. The game resembled soccer, except that the players were mounted on horseback and the ball was five or six feet in diameter. One cowboy who often played remembered,

> The game was little short of murder. Those redskins were out to win, and with a couple of tons of horse meat bringing that six-foot ball at top speed to try and put it past Cy Compton, our goalkeeper, we

Pawnee Bill (left) and Buffalo Bill (right) joined forces in 1909 to produce Buffalo Bill's Wild West and Pawnee Bill's Far East Combined. Pawnee Bill further internationalized the scope of Cody's show by bringing in Australian, Chinese, and East Indian performers.

cowhands came to have a heap of respect for it. Robert Little Dog usually was goalkeeper on the Indian side and it was next to impossible to put the ball past his big mount. The crippling came when both teams were pushing and the ball caught a toe or a kneecap as it ground by.[35]

Even a man who did stunt bicycling was given a billing in keeping with the idea of the Wild West. His name was George C. Davis, but he was better known as the "Cowboy Cyclist."

Parades

Wild West shows, however, offered more than simply a sequence of acts in a portable arena. Nearly every Wild West show of any size began with a parade down the main streets of the town. The parade was free. It served as an ad-

vertisement for the show, and it was a way of extending good will to the community. For a large show such as the 101 Ranch or Buffalo Bill's Wild West, these parades were elaborate indeed. "Grand Street Cavalcade on the Morning of Exhibition," Cody advertised in a Kansas newspaper. "Passing Through Principal Streets, Leaving the Grounds at 9.30 O'clock."[36]

As time went on, outfits tried to outdo each other in the length and magic of their parades. The 101 Ranch used forty different wagons in theirs, including a bandwagon with wood engravings on each side; one observer remarked that it "could not be duplicated at any price."[37] Cody's bandwagon may not have been so beautiful, but required eight horses to pull it. In addition, parades often featured calliopes, bands, animals, and at least some of the featured performers.

For most large shows and many smaller ones, admission also allowed interested people

"$9,000 a Week in Wages"

Although Wild West shows could be put on for very little money, at least in comparison to a circus, a large Wild West show was a very expensive undertaking. Nate Salsbury gave a newspaper reporter some idea of the costs in an 1892 interview, quoted in Sarah Blackstone's book, *Buckskins, Bullets, and Business: A History of Buffalo Bill's Wild West*:

"You would want $150,000 as a start, and as you are inexperienced in the business it would probably take you a year to get all your people and animals together. . . . You would need 30 people—Indians, cowboys, Mexicans, etc. and be prepared to pay $9,000 a week in wages. . . . You must ad-

vertise. We keep forty men out posting. In six months we will have spent from $750,000 to $875,000 in advertising. . . . There's the cost of a thousand loads of cinder to put down on the ground. You would have to buy 300 lbs. of paint to put on your big canvas scene at the back, and by-the-bye, there is the canvas for over 40 tents in which your company sleep. Of course you would not want to stay in the same place for good, so if you cared to make a railroad journey to another spot with your show, just book 95 carriages and wagons. Take your own portable grandstand—that costs $25,000."

It took many sold-out shows to justify expenses like that.

Upon entering the town in which they will perform, members of Cody's Wild West show give townspeople a preview of what's to come.

to wander the grounds of the show, looking at various exhibits and examining the livestock and guns. Touring replica Indian villages seems to have been an especially popular attraction for audiences. Some shows had their actors do double duty, appearing also in small demonstrations outside the arena before showtime: crafts, dancing, storytelling, discussions of weapons, and the like. Other shows had band members play to entertain early arrivals, and a few advertised circus-style sideshows including bearded ladies, snake charmers, and lion tamers.

Wild West shows varied significantly in the specifics of the acts they presented. Moreover, from one year to the next, few, if any, productions stayed the same. Most promoters were constantly looking for ways to fine-tune their shows and make them ever more appealing to audiences. Yet at the same time Wild West shows had plenty in common. The themes of guns, horses, cowboys, and Native Americans predominated in nearly every show ever put together. Wild West shows featured shooters, ropers, riders, and Western dramas; even when they moved away from these themes, they moved in predictable ways. Whatever the year and the company, Wild West shows were unmistakable.

The Performers

A large Wild West show was an enormous undertaking. Buffalo Bill's production often encompassed six or seven hundred people, including cast members, crew, and support personnel. One or two other shows reached a number closer to a thousand. Even the smaller shows included people of very different backgrounds, outlooks, and reasons for performing. Moreover, the experiences of white American performers were different from the experiences of the foreign riders and marksmen who joined the bigger shows, and both groups differed even more from the Indians.

For this reason, it is difficult to make generalizations about the people who joined Wild West shows. Some performers were genuine Westerners; others were not. Some had ex-

tensive backgrounds in theater or circuses; others did not. A few joined the Wild West because it was the best available job, others signed on because they had loved the real West, and still others were after money or adventure. Now and then a performer became a star and spent many years with a show, but most lasted only a season or two on tour.

Cowboys

Nearly all shows advertised cowboys and featured them frequently during the program. Fortunately, recruiting cowboys was not especially difficult for most companies. Cody had no trouble finding all the men he needed when he began his tour. The Miller Brothers "ransacked

This photograph of the cast of Buffalo Bill's Wild West show reveals the immensity of the production.

A cowboy attempts to break a bronco. Buffalo Bill had no problem luring such men away from ranching to join his Wild West shows.

the great Southwest"[38] to hire exactly the men they wanted. Both Cody and the Millers liked to advertise that all their performers were genuine Westerners. While this statement may have been an exaggeration, it contained a lot of truth. Once in a while professional actors, or athletic men from from the East who were looking for adventure, took on the roles of show cowboys, but it was far more common for actual cowboys to play rodeo parts.

Attracting cowboys was easy for many reasons. Perhaps the most important was economics. Cody offered cowboys a salary of sixty dollars a month in 1883 if they would join his show. Sixty dollars was significantly higher than the salary a man might earn by working in a textile mill or coal mine. It was also an improvement on the wages of most cowboys. While not all shows paid what Cody offered, most were close enough to make the money worthwhile.

And as time went on, Wild West salaries began to look even more inviting. By the turn of the century, barbed wire was prevalent across the West. Many acres of prairie land had been fenced off, with cattle grazing freely within them. The days of the long cat-

tle drives were coming to an end. Cowboys were in less demand than ever. With so many men unemployed or underemployed, it was common for cowhands to turn to Wild West shows for an opportunity. The files of the Miller Brothers 101 Ranch Wild West show, for example, bulged with letters from cowboys eager for a job.

Except for a handful of stars, however, few cowboys stayed for long with any show. Indeed, Cody routinely invited more cowhands to join his show each year than he had room for. He anticipated that some who had expressed interest would back out, or would change their minds after a few days in camp, and he was right. Many of the cowboys who did sign on for a tour returned to ranch life after a year or so. Some said they found it more exciting and rewarding to do "real" work. The Miller Brothers shuffled cowboys back and forth between their Wild West show and their 101 Ranch in northern Oklahoma. "The exuberant young men who struggled with the bucking bronco for the amusement of the public one day," wrote an observer, "might be branding calves on the ranges of the 101 Ranch the next week."[39]

The Performers

Managing a Wild West show was complicated. Successful Wild West shows needed not only performers and backstage staff, but also required men in positions such as business manager, publicity agent, and general manager. Someone needed to purchase food, pay performers, book arenas, and coordinate advertising. In some smaller shows the owners or organizers doubled in all administrative capacities, but larger shows hired extra staff. Records from 1886 show that Cody and Salsbury, for instance, had eight managers in addition to themselves. Fifteen years later, this group had almost doubled in size.

Probably the most famous administrator was John Burke. Born in Washington, D.C., Burke got his start working as a reporter, an actor, and a theatrical agent. He met Cody during Cody's career in melodrama. The two men became friends, and Burke signed up as general manager for Cody's first season. He enjoyed it so much he came back every year until the show merged with Pawnee Bill's in 1913.

Though he was called a general manager, Burke was perhaps better described as a press agent. He wrote programs and advertisements, and he also talked newspaper editors into writing stories about Cody and the show. He was quite successful at his job. Burke came to adopt a Western manner, calling himself "Major" or "Arizona John," although historians believe he had never been west of the Missouri River until Cody began his show.

Like Burke, most other Wild West managers had theatrical backgrounds, not Western experience. Jules Keen, Cody's treasurer for many years, had been a melodrama actor. He had also performed one year with the Wild West show before taking over the accounts. Albert Scheible took on the business manager's job for Cody in 1894; before that he, too, had been a theater manager.

Burke's lack of Western background concerned Cody not at all, nor did it bother Pawnee Bill when he joined forces with Cody years later. Don Russell, in his book *The Lives and Legends of Buffalo Bill*, quotes Pawnee Bill noting that Burke "knew more managing editors and owners of big publications, and called them by their first names, than any man who ever lived." Curiously, Burke *did* grate on Nate Salsbury, the one man of the three whose background was most like Burke's own. Russell cites Salsbury's opinion that Burke was more interested in self-promotion than anything else. "I do not believe there is another man in the world in his position," Salsbury griped, "that would have had the gall to exploit himself at the expense of the show as much as John Burke!"

While returning to the range was the most common next step for cowboys, not all followed this pattern. A few men, seeing the East and Midwest for the first time, decided to stay. They settled in cities and towns, occasionally marrying women they met along the road. Some cowboys did the opposite. They plunged into show business with a passion. Guy Weadick, a performer in the 101 Ranch Wild West show, was a founder of the Calgary Stampede, one of the world's most famous rodeos. And William Levi "Buck" Taylor not only opened his own Wild West show after a few seasons spent as head cowboy under Cody, he also managed Denver's Cowboy Tournament in 1890.

Taylor was perhaps the first cowboy hero. Born in Texas in 1857, he was an orphan before the age of ten. He said once,

I was dependent on myself at an age when ordinary children are still in the nursery. There was only one thing to do, which was to be a cowpuncher. . . . By the time I was 14 I was able to ride and rope with some of the best of them and was known around our section as the best cowpuncher of my age that had ever been seen.[40]

In the West of the late nineteenth century, cowpunching was the obvious choice for a boy of Taylor's strength, determination, and competitive drive. Before long he was living and working on Cody's ranch in North Platte. When Cody opened his Wild West show, he invited Taylor to join him, and Taylor agreed. He saw show business as the next natural ex-

Cowboy hero William Levi "Buck" Taylor managed to overcome childhood adversity to found his own Wild West show and become manager of Denver's Cowboy Tournament.

tension of his talents and abilities. According to Cody's programs, Taylor was "amiable as a child,"[41] even though he had remarkable strength and courage. Later on, Taylor became the hero of many dime novels, just like Buffalo Bill himself.

Another famous Wild West performer was Bill Pickett. Many cowboys were African Americans, but Pickett was probably the only one to become a headliner in a Wild West show. Born in 1863 in Williamson County, Texas, Pickett is generally credited with inventing the sport of bulldogging, or wrestling a long-horned steer to the ground. According to a contemporary account, Pickett developed bulldogging in self-defense. While riding patrol on a Texas ranch, Pickett looked up to discover a steer about to gore his horse. Thinking fast, Pickett slid off his horse, "hooked [the] steer with both hands on the horns, twisted its neck and then sunk his teeth in the steer's nostrils to bring him down."[42]

Although he eventually gave up on the biting, Pickett did go on to be a champion bulldogger and a star for the 101 Ranch Wild West show for many years. As with Taylor, Pickett could make better money by Wild Westing than by remaining a cowboy. Pickett also had the disadvantage of being black at a time when many rodeo contests were not willing to allow nonwhite performers.

Loyalty and Friendship

Friendship was another important reason performers joined Wild West shows. Cody had connections with cowboys and other Westerners gained from years of exploring, hunting, and scouting, and he encouraged men he had worked with to come work for him. Many did. The first Wild West show, for instance, included not only Buck Taylor, but

Major Frank North, frontier scout Con Groner, and trapper John Y. Nelson, who brought along his Sioux wife and their children when he joined up. Cody also attracted several former Pony Express riders, most of whom he knew personally, to take part in a demonstration of carrying the mail.

These men joined Cody's show partly because of loyalty and friendship, but also because the work was sometimes easier than what they were used to. Of course, touring with a Wild West show was no vacation. Travel was hard and the work often taxing. Bulldogging could be downright dangerous. So could bronco busting, as this account indicates:

When a bronco out on the ranges of the West, by bad handling becomes thoroughly vicious, has earned the name of the "Colorado Cloudburst," or the "Dakota Demon," the "Montana Man-Killer," or some such reassuring title, and there is not a bronco buster on the range who will tackle him, and he is not worth two trade dollars to anyone, they ship him to a "Wild West" show.[43]

But to men accustomed to fighting Indians, driving cattle hundreds of miles across deserts, or tracking elk through snow-covered mountains, Wild West shows seemed much less demanding. Wild West employees were given food and sleeping accommodations, and their personal safety was a much surer thing than it had been in the Old West. For some older men, in particular, the Wild West shows offered a chance to show off their remaining skills in a less demanding environment.

Other cowboys, however, joined precisely because they wanted adventure. At its best, a Wild West show promised its cast members excitement, drama, and travel. Some had never been off the Plains or beyond the borders of Western states. Others had grown tired of the same old routines of ranch life. They wanted something more, and hoped that the touring Wild West show would provide it. Certainly the prospect of visiting the big cities of the East, traveling by special train car, meeting new people, and perhaps even crossing the Atlantic Ocean to Europe was a big draw for many of the younger cowboys.

Cowgirls

Like the cowboys who joined Wild West shows, the cowgirls who signed on were looking for many things: adventure, money, excitement, and perhaps more. Again like the cowboys, most women in Wild West shows came from the West, grew up in rural areas, and had little formal education. They benefited from living in a culture where, as one historian describes it, "athleticism, skill, competitiveness, and grit were acceptable traits for women."[44] Like their male counterparts, women in the West were expected to be tough.

There was one major difference between cowgirls and cowboys, however. The job market for women who wanted to work anywhere but their own ranch was limited. That made joining Wild West shows extremely attractive to ambitious young women, and to those who had no ranch of their own and wanted to work with horses and cattle.

The most famous woman rider, and the one who helped to popularize the term "cowgirl," was Lucille Mulhall. Mulhall was born in St. Louis on October 21, 1885, but her family soon moved to an Oklahoma ranch. From an early age, she loved to rope and to ride. Before she was twelve she was a Wild West performer; by 1900 she was a featured star. Audiences admired her skills. A New York newspaper reported,

Famed cowgirl and performer Lucille Mulhall waits to take her turn at a steer roping competition in 1905. Mulhall began performing in Wild West shows as a child.

Little Miss Mulhall, who weighs only 90 pounds, can break a bronco, lasso and brand a steer and shoot a coyote at 500 yards. She can also play Chopin, quote Browning, construe Vergil, and make mayonnaise dressing. She is a little ashamed of these latter accomplishments, which are a concession to the civilized prejudices of her mother.[45]

Most other cowgirls, such as Lulu Belle Parr and Florence LaDue, likewise grew up with Western backgrounds and found Wild West shows a logical career move. A British reviewer of the Miller Brothers show stated that "the majority of the girls are the daughters and sisters of small ranchers," and went on to add, not quite accurately, that "all the feats they perform are practically part of every-day ranch life."[46]

But not every cowgirl followed this path. Some cowgirls got to Wild West shows without having Western roots. Many of these joined over the objection of their families. "Prairie Lillie" Allen, for instance, was born in Tennessee and grew up in Chicago. As a teenager, she visited Dubrock's Wild West Show and loved it. She joined the show to ride the broncos, but wore a mask so parents and friends would not recognize her. Allen went on to become a rodeo performer after leaving the Wild West circuit.

An even more remarkable story belonged to Tillie Baldwin. Born in Norway, Baldwin moved to the United States at age eighteen, lived with an aunt, and became a hairdresser. One day she saw a group of women doing riding tricks in a local park. Baldwin decided she wanted to learn them too. Through a combination of lessons and diligent work on her own she learned enough to get a job in a small Wild West show. By 1912 she had worked her way up to being a star performer for the 101 Ranch.

Sharpshooters

Except possibly for Cody himself, no Wild West performer was more famous or popular than sharpshooter Annie Oakley. Born Phoebe Ann Moses on August 13, 1860, in Darke County, Ohio, Oakley grew up in poverty. She started her shooting career while quite young. As she once told an interviewer,

I was eight years old when I made my first shot, and I still consider it one of the best shots I ever made. I saw a squirrel run down over the grass in front of the house, through the orchard and stop on the fence to get a hickory nut. I decided to shoot it and ran into the house to get a gun which was hanging on the wall and which I knew to be loaded. I was so little I had to jump up on a chair and slide it down to the mantel and then to the ground. I laid the gun on the railing of the porch, and then recalled that I had heard my brother say about shooting, "It is a disgrace to shoot a squirrel anywhere but in the head because it spoils the meat to hit him elsewhere." I took the remark literally and decided, in a flash, that I must hit that squirrel in the head, or be disgraced. It was a wonderful shot, going right through the head from side to side.[47]

It was almost Oakley's last shot. Her mother forbade her to touch the gun for the next eight months. But Oakley was persistent. More to the point, she rarely missed. Before long she was the family hunter. Without her ability to shoot accurately, her family might have starved.

Oakley often sold excess game to a hotelkeeper in Cincinnati. He in turn set up a shooting match between her and a professional marksman named Frank Butler. Oakley outshot him. She married him a year later and they toured the country as the shooting act of Butler and Oakley. After playing variety shows, circuses, and county fairs, Oakley decided to

An early photograph of famed markswoman Annie Oakley shows her in Wild West regalia. Growing up in poverty, Oakley's phenomenal accuracy with a gun allowed her to consistently provide food for her family.

try out for Cody's Wild West shortly after it had opened. Though Cody and Salsbury were dubious at first, they signed her up after watching her shoot. She usually appeared second on the program, right after the "Grand Review" parade of soldiers from various armies around the world. The program referred to Oakley as a "Celebrated Shot, who will illustrate her dexterity in the use of Fire-arms."[48]

Oakley's tricks were remarkable, all the more so as she was a very small woman. As part of the act, she had Butler hold a dime between his thumb and forefinger. Backing up thirty paces, Oakley shot the coin out of his grip without hitting him. Assistants threw playing cards into the air, and Oakley would riddle them with bullet holes before they hit the earth. Some of Oakley's other demonstrations included shooting with the rifle held upside down on her head; firing at moving targets while pedaling around the arena on a bicycle; and using three different shotguns to shoot six balls, all thrown into the air at the same time.

There were other well-known shooters, too. May Manning Lillie of Pawnee Bill's show was known as the "Champion Girl Shot of the West" even though she was born and raised in eastern Pennsylvania. Lillian Smith joined Cody's show at the age of fifteen. Cody himself was noted for his shooting accuracy. So was Johnnie Baker, whom Cody billed as a "Celebrated Young American Marksman." Baker was best known for his unorthodox shooting positions. He was especially famous for standing on his head while aiming at targets. An assistant steadied his legs so he could grip the gun. Cody's shows often included a competition between Oakley and Baker. Oakley always won. There was suspicion at the time that the result was staged, but Baker said years later that Oakley was simply a better shot. "It would have made a better show if I could have beaten her every few performances," he admitted. "But it couldn't be done."[49]

Foreign Performers

Just as not all "Western" performers were actually from the West, not all "foreign" performers were truly foreign either. If Cossacks or Mexicans were needed only in crowd scenes, promoters often hired white cowboys to take the roles, wearing appropriate cos-

tumes. The expense of bringing in true foreigners was too high. Occasionally a cowboy would pass himself off as a non-English speaker for an entire tour, but it was more common to assign parts as they were needed. In some cases, moreover, the people supposedly being represented were fictional. Cody advertised a "Feejee Indian from Africa," even though Fiji is many thousands of miles from Africa and neither Fijians nor Africans are called Indians. In reality, the role was played by a black American cowboy.

But as with the American cowboys, foreign riders were not especially hard to attract. Some of the Cossacks who performed

A poster advertises the unusual shooting positions favored by marksman Johnnie Baker.

The Cowboy Band

Like the foreign horsemen, the musicians hired by Wild West shows may not always have been quite as advertised. A page from an early Cody program claims that the Cowboy Band was "organized from those Cowboys who have cultivated a natural talent for music to while away the idle hours of camp life." It was a good story. In fact, cowboys *were* noted for their music. Singing provided several functions during cattle drives. Songs could help relax and calm the cowboys after a long day on the trail. Songs also quieted the cattle, especially at night, and could help shield sounds that might otherwise cause a stampede. Many cowboy songs were already well known during the late nineteenth century and have gained in popularity since then.

But in truth, most of the thirty-plus members of Buffalo Bill's Cowboy Band were not cowboys at all. They were professional musicians from the East, mainly young men who took the job because it was the best they could get in their field. The only exception was Colonel William Sweeney, the band leader, a Westerner who was an old friend of Cody's. Indeed, Sweeney was the only one of the musicians who lasted for long with the show. Sweeney was well paid, but the other musicians received a wage that was adequate at best. In 1910, for instance, most of the band members earned just a little more than the $11 a week the average American worker took home.

Whenever possible, Cody had his musicians play while mounted on horseback. They wore moccasins, gray shirts, and slouched hats. Band members were on call perhaps more often than any other performer. Not only were they responsible for the overture (typically the Star-Spangled Banner) and incidental music during the program, they also performed in street parades, and they frequently played classical music, popular songs, and cowboy dance tunes before and after shows. Mostly this music was well received. Michael Masterson, in his *Sounds of the Frontier: Music in Buffalo Bill's Wild West*, quotes a London *Times* reporter on the Cowboy Band: "They give a concert before each performance, and incidental music that is a source of pleasure to all who hear it, and are daily greeted with rounds of applause."

Members of the Wild West show's band pose for a photograph. Although billed as cowboys, who had honed their talents on the range, most of Cody's band was composed of professional musicians.

in Cody's shows were lured by the money. Indeed, the Wild West pay scale was much higher than what most foreigners could command in their own countries. Others were happy to escape from political troubles or wars back home. As they sought cowboys, Wild West shows seem to have sought out foreign performers, too. Cody, for instance, sent an agent named C. M. Ercole to find a suitable group of Cossacks. Later, he did the same with South American riders. And once several members of a culture had experienced Wild West shows, word of mouth helped recruit others.

The Cossacks were probably the most famous and compelling of the foreign performers. According to Cody, his first group of Cossacks were the first ever to leave Russia to perform elsewhere. Whether this is true is unknown. The Cossacks were noted for unusual riding skills, such as the ability to ride while facing either forwards or backwards. Many of them also rode while standing on their head. A Cody program advertised,

> In the Russian Cossack [Cody and Salsbury] found a horseman whose style was new, novel and striking, and one who could compete with the finest in the world. These Cossacks, in the picturesque garb of the Caucasus, form the latest acquisition of the Wild West.[50]

Audiences did indeed find the Cossacks "striking" and "picturesque," though not everyone liked them equally. One newspaper reviewer dismissed their traditional folk dance as "skipping about in an idiotic manner."[51]

Unfortunately, very little is known about most of the men and the few women who came to Wild West shows from outside the United States. Some, such as lasso expert Vincente Oropeza, stayed in Wild West shows for many years, eventually attaining top billing. Oropeza had been recruited by Cody. He was already a champion roper and had performed often in Mexico. A few others, including a Lebanese acrobat named George Hamid who performed with Cody's show, gave up Wild Westing after a while but remained in America. In Hamid's case, he stayed in show business, becoming a producer in New Jersey. But the majority of performers fulfilled their contracts and then went home. Once in a while they left under unpleasant circumstances. Alexis Lucca, a Cossack who had brought his countrymen to several different Wild West shows, returned to Russia with his group when the First World War broke out. He was never heard from again.

Wild West show participants came from many different backgrounds and joined for all kinds of reasons. Despite their differences, however, they helped create a unique American entertainment. More than anyone, these performers *were* the Wild West shows. Without their backgrounds, experiences, and contributions, the shows would never have begun. From the performers who made a career out of Wild Westing down to the many cast members who spent only a season or so on tour, they all helped make the Wild West what it was.

Native Americans

A Wild West show could have all the Cossacks, cowgirls, lariats, and bucking broncos there were and yet not be successful. Much as audiences flocked to see these attractions, there was one group that people wanted to see more than any other: American Indians. Nearly every show of any size had at least a few Indians who participated in the show in some way, whether demonstrating riding feats, playing the role of a bloodthirsty warrior, or simply adding exotic, Western flavor to Eastern audiences. And the larger shows had many Native Americans—sometimes up to half the total cast.

The Indian experience, however, was not the same as the experiences of the cowboys, sharpshooters, or even the foreign recruits. Indians came to shows in very different ways from whites. They were not treated by audiences or management in precisely the same way as their white counterparts, either. Moreover, unlike white Americans, who could take on several different roles during a tour, Indians were more or less restricted to playing themselves.

Reservations

By the time Cody set up his first Wild West show, the wars between Native Americans and the U.S. army were drawing to a close. Although a few skirmishes were still to come, notably in the Southwest and on the northern Great Plains, the Indians had lost. Several

Native Americans were staples of the Wild West shows, but because most lived on reservations, hiring them was sometimes difficult.

decades of fighting between whites and Indians had led to the claiming of most of the West for white settlers, and the removal of most Indians to sections of unwanted land called reservations.

For the most part, life on the reservations was bleak. Indians who had followed the buffalo for food could no longer do so. Not only were they banned from areas that had once been part of their hunting grounds, but the buffalo was rapidly becoming scarce, hunted almost to extinction by white sportsmen. Many Native Americans had died, the victims of war,

The most unusual route any Indians took to Wild West shows occurred in 1891. The last main battle between Indians and whites had taken place in Wounded Knee, South Dakota, late in 1890. Many Indians had been killed, and about twenty Sioux men had been taken prisoners of war. They were shipped first to the prison at Fort Sheridan, Illinois, and then were released into the custody of William Cody and his Wild West show. Along with about a hundred other Indians, the prisoners immediately traveled to Europe to perform there.

The decision made sense on several levels. From the government's point of view, it took the prisoners far from their homes and made a repeat of the uprising less likely. It also saved taxpayers money, as Cody took on the responsibility of clothing and feeding the prisoners. Moreover, the release worked for Cody and the prisoners themselves.

Cody could advertise ferocious Indians, recently arrested in connection with the Indian wars, and make extra money. Meanwhile, the prisoners could avoid jail time.

But some reformers were outraged. Those who disliked Wild West shows were especially annoyed. They argued that joining a show was not in the best interests of any Indian, especially not Indians who had been so recently involved in violence. Moreover, they felt, the message that the government was sending was the wrong one. One reformer, quoted in L. C. Moses' book, *Wild West Shows and the Images of the American Indian*, complained that releasing the prisoners was rewarding them for "treason, thieving, and possibly murder, while the peaceable man remains at home in poverty." Their efforts were fruitless, however. The decision stood.

famine, or disease, which not only reduced numbers but disrupted social structures as well.

A white agent governed each reservation, and the agents were answerable to various offices in the federal government. While agents had limited power—after an 1879 court decision, for instance, they could not legally prevent an Indian from leaving the reservation if he or she so chose—in practice their word was law. Few people, Indian or white, made moves on a reservation without consulting either the local agent or his superiors.

Hiring Show Indians

Hiring Indians for Wild West shows, then, was more complicated than hiring cowboys or sharpshooters. A white rider could be easily

recruited: a letter or visit would do the trick. But to hire Indians, managers generally had to go through Indian agents and their bosses. By 1886, the Indian Bureau had published regulations about the employment of Indians in Wild West shows. Whether requesting a specific leader or simply a group of twenty or a hundred Indians, promoters had to promise, as Cody did in 1893,

to pay the Indians for their services a fair compensation, to furnish them proper food and clothing, to pay their traveling and needful incidental expenses from the date of leaving the agencies until their return thereto, to protect them from all immoral influences and surroundings, to provide all needful medical attendance and medicine, to do everything that may

The government had final say over whether Native Americans could join Wild West shows. When Cody requested that he be able to hire famed chief Sitting Bull (pictured), the government initially refused his request.

be requisite for their health, comfort, and welfare, and to return the Indians to their reservations within the time specified by the Interior Department without charge or cost to them.[52]

Even with these promises, requests were not usually accepted without a fight. When Cody asked for permission to hire Sioux leader Sitting Bull as a star attraction, the Secretary of the Interior instructed the local Indian agent to "Make a *very* emphatic *No!*," and underlined the word "No" three times.[53] As far as the government was concerned, Indians should be improving themselves on their reservations, not "roving through the country exhibiting themselves and visiting places where they would naturally come into contact with evil associates and degrading immoralities."[54] Cody had to write back attesting to his own good character and giving his personal assurance that Sitting Bull would not be corrupted. Only then did the government give him permission to hire Sitting Bull.

Other promoters ran into the same problems. "I don't allow Indians to join Wild West shows," said a Montana agent shortly after the restrictions went into effect.[55] In 1892, government official Thomas Jefferson Morgan denied the request of Doc Carver's company to hire several Sioux. Moreover, he told the Indians that if they joined the show anyway and were stranded far from home, they could expect no government help. The Office of Indian Affairs approved only two requests to hire Indians during the year 1893. While it was possible to hire Indians without the permission of the government—and some shows did—it was more comfortable for everyone if permission could be obtained.

The government looked most favorably on shows that seemed to be for educational as well as entertainment purposes. Cody, who billed his show as a mix of history and instruction, generally got what he wanted, though not without a struggle. During the late 1890s, the Indian Bureau gave full backing to a show called the Indian Congress, which exhibited Indians from at least thirty different tribes; its fans called it "not a Wild West show, but a serious ethnological exhibition."[56] As for shows that simply re-created battles, most Indian agents felt they were not only immoral but also dangerous. "The Indian has greatly lost by such employment," said Indian agent Daniel Dorchester. "He is taught to renew the wildest and most savage scenes of Indian warfare."[57] Dorchester and others feared that Native Americans would be tempted to start battles again if they were featured in these Wild West shows.

"We Were Raised on Horseback"

In fact, many Indians were pleased to join a Wild West show. Reservation life was difficult, and young men, in particular, jumped at the chance to go elsewhere. As with cowboys, part of the reason for this was money. On the reservations jobs besides farming were scarce. Even farming was often impossible, since the most fertile land had been claimed by white settlers. The wages Indians could earn in a Wild West show were far above what most could make staying home. In the Wild West shows of the 1890s, for instance, Indians were typically paid about twenty-five dollars a month. This was very little in comparison with what cowboys or sharpshooters were offered, but was better than an Indian could hope for in any other line of work.

Other Indians, however, were less interested in the money. As Daniel Dorchester feared, they wanted to re-create the lives they had known—although not necessarily with hostile intent. "We were raised on horseback; that is the way we had to work," Black Heart explained when asked why he had joined Cody and Salsbury's show. "These men furnished us the same work we were raised to."[58] Although the government had tried to forbid Indians from doing war dances on the reservation, the Indians of the 101 Ranch Wild West were allowed to perform them as part of the show. Ironically, the best way for Indians to reclaim pieces of their heritage was to leave the reservation to play themselves or their ancestors for white people.

Another common reason for joining Wild West shows was adventure. Many Indians who joined had never been off their reservations. They had heard stories of cities, oceans, and different peoples and applied to Wild West shows as a way of broadening their hori-

The Chicago World's Fair

Perhaps the best experience Wild West Indians had was with Cody's show in 1893, when the company spent most of the season in Chicago at the World's Fair. Indians were generally allowed to go where they wanted when on tour, but language and cultural barriers made it hard to do much, especially when the show was moving on a daily or almost-daily basis. The extended stay in Chicago, though, was different. Records from the show indicate that the Indians spent quite a bit of time touring the city and taking boat rides on Lake Michigan.

The Indians particularly loved the fair, too. The World's Fair of that year, also called the Columbian Exposition, featured many exhibits of culture and many more of sheer entertainment. The Indians' favorite part of the fair seems to have been the merry-go-round. A Chicago newspaper reported that fifteen Sioux once boarded the carousel together; then, as it picked up speed, grabbed the reins of their horses in both their hands and gave full-throated yells. These Indians, said the newspaper, quoted in L. C. Moses' book, *Wild West Shows and the Images of the American Indian*, "seem to like being jerked around on a carousel. They prefer it to art galleries, and some people who are not Indians feel the same way."

zons. They were not disappointed, although the changes were sometimes overwhelming. "I see so much that is wonderful and strange," said American Horse, who joined Cody's show in 1886, "that I feel a wish sometimes to go out in the forest and cover my head with a blanket, so that I can see no more and have a chance to think over what I have seen."[59]

Often, Indians who were motivated by traveling were especially anxious to learn more about white people and their ways. Some were hoping for knowledge that would help them restore things as they had been before the coming of the whites. "Maybe if I could see the sacred world of the Wasichu [whites]," said Black Elk, "I could understand how to bring the sacred hoop together and make the tree to bloom again at the center of it."[60] Others were hoping to learn from white society. "The red man is changing every season," said Red Shirt, who accompanied Cody's troupe to England. "Our children will learn the white man's civilization and to live like him."[61]

The People

While many Indian tribes sent members to Wild West shows, one group stands out: the Sioux. Cody preferred to work with Sioux whenever possible. In his opinion, Sioux were "more hardy than the others," though he singled out a few other tribes that he considered almost equal to them.[62] On one tour, the program listed each Sioux performer by name, and then noted that "52 Pawnee and Wichita braves" would also be performing.[63]

Again, Cody set the standard. Various branches of the Sioux accounted for many more Wild West Indians, in Cody's show and out, than any other tribe. Even shows based in the Southwest, far from Sioux reservations,

hired Sioux when they could. Joe Miller, of the 101 Ranch Wild West, for instance, believed that the local Oklahoma Ponca and Osage Indians lacked discipline and drive. "Most of them," agreed an observer, "tire of show life."[64]

It helped that the most famous Western battles had involved the Sioux: Custer's Last Stand, the Battle of Wounded Knee, and many others. Before the year 1900, the popular urban image of a Native American was the Plains Indian in general and the Sioux in particular. Shows that did hire Apaches, Comanches, or Utes often had them dress in the distinctive Sioux way, especially when performing out of the country. And when pro-

Cody (pictured) went to great lengths to recruit Native Americans to join his show, knowing that they were the main attraction for most of his audiences.

Perhaps the stickiest issue regarding Indians who performed in Wild West shows was the availability of liquor. When Cody promised to keep his Indian employees away from "immoral influences and surroundings," he knew those were code words for liquor stores and bars. Several observers took it for granted that money paid to Indians would be wasted on gambling, women, and, especially, alcohol.

While this was an exaggeration, liquor *was* a problem for Wild West shows, and perhaps especially for Indians. One man fell between the cars of a moving train and was killed; he had been drunk at the time. Others had to be sent home because of constant drunkenness. It was easy for the Indians to purchase beer and other alcoholic drinks on their own. Moreover, especially in Europe, locals often treated them to all the drinks they wanted.

No one worried more about the problem than Luther Standing Bear. In his autobiography, *My People the Sioux*, Standing Bear described his trip to Europe with Cody's show. Before they left the United States, Standing Bear called a meeting at which he told the other Sioux:

"My relations, you all know that I am to take care of you while going across the big water to another country, and all the time we are to stay there. I have heard that when any one joins this show, about the first thing he thinks of is getting drunk. I understand that

the regulations of the Buffalo Bill show require that no Indian shall be given any liquor. You all know that I do not drink, and I am going to keep you all from it. Don't think that because you may be closely related to me I will shield you, for I will not. I will report to Colonel Cody immediately any one I find drinking."

Liquor did turn out to be a problem, and Standing Bear had to be ever alert. He developed a sign-out system to keep track of who was leaving the grounds and where they were going. Later he held a portion of wages back to make sure that the Indians in his custody did not have enough money to buy liquor on their own. Some of the Indians were creative in their attempts to get alcohol. Standing Bear wrote,

"During the rainy weather, some of them thought they had an excuse to drink. They said they thought it kept them warm. I saw at once that this must not go on, as a little whiskey always calls for more."

But for the most part, Standing Bear's vigilance paid off. He caught three Sioux with a bottle of whiskey one day. Cody decided not to punish them for the first offense, but the message had been sent. "If I remember correctly," Standing Bear wrote, "we did not have any further trouble with the Indians about liquor while in London."

---

moters wanted members of different tribes for variety's sake, they were apt to hire more Sioux and pass them off as Cheyennes or Kiowas. "While all the Indians belonged to the Sioux tribe," wrote Luther Standing Bear, an interpreter with Cody's company, "we were

supposed to represent four different tribes, each tribe to ride animals of one color."[65]

The Indian Bureau urged show promoters to hire married Indian men and have them bring their wives or entire families along. Single men, agents reasoned, would be more

The public was greatly drawn to the Native American women and children members of the Wild West shows.

likely to create havoc on tour. Wives would help keep their husbands in line. Many Indian women did accompany their husbands. In fact, promoters quickly realized that adding women and children helped make their shows more attractive than ever. Cody included women in several acts of his show, paying them roughly the same wages as the men.

But Indian women did not have to be performers to make the shows seem even more realistic. Indian women were a big draw for people who toured the grounds of the show before the program began. An observer of the Miller Brothers Wild West show wrote,

> In the Indian village that existed in connection with the show, the Indians were seen as they were in the wilds, not alone for exhibition purposes, but because they preferred it. The squaws were expert makers of bead-work, blankets, baskets, and pottery. The bucks made bows and arrows and would sit for hours, carving

out some weird design, without looking up, or saying a word.[66]

The Indian children were even more of an attraction. The 101 Ranch considered Indian children perhaps the most exciting sight of its show. Red Shirt's wife gave birth to a baby boy while Cody's company was touring Europe. When the news was announced in the arena, there was much applause and excitement. Several years later, Cody toured England again. This time, a baby was born to Luther Standing Bear and his wife. On Cody's request, they allowed their newborn daughter to be exhibited as part of the show:

> Long before it was time for the show to begin, people were lining up in the road. My wife sat on a raised platform, with the little one in the cradle before her. The people filed past, many of them dropping money in a box for her. Nearly every one had some sort of little gift for her also. It

was a great drawing card for the show; the work was very light for my wife, and as for the baby, before she was twenty-four hours old she was making more money than my wife and I together.[67]

Cody preferred to work with Indians whose contact with whites had been limited. In some cases, however, promoters made exceptions. There were a number of educated Indians who, like Luther Standing Bear, had learned English and knew something of life off the reservation. These "assimilated" Indians were considered especially easy to work with. Walter Battice, for example, was a Sac and Fox Indian who joined the Miller Brothers show. He spent his days off traveling and exploring; he visited Washington, New York, and several other places on his own. "Rates on the water are very cheap to all points on the coast," he wrote to a friend from Norfolk, Virginia, "so one can go to all the larger Cities for little money after once getting here."[68] Another assimilated Indian wrote to the Millers for employment; he had short hair but added that he owned Indian wigs.

Sitting Bull and Black Elk

The list of Indians who were given feature billing at Wild West shows is long. While most of the names are forgotten today, many were once as well known as a star baseball player or movie actor might be now. Among the famous Indian leaders who appeared at some point were Geronimo, Red Cloud, Young Man Afraid of His Horses, Black Elk, and Sitting Bull.

Of these, Sitting Bull is no doubt the most familiar name today. Leader of the Hunkpapa Sioux, Sitting Bull was involved in the Battle of Little Big Horn. He toured twice with Wild West shows, the second time with Cody's. Cody included a picture of himself and Sitting Bull in his show's program booklet with the caption "Foes in '76—Friends in '85,"[69] but the real draw was the fact that Sitting Bull was responsible for George Armstrong Custer's death.

Indeed, attendance soared when Cody brought Sitting Bull into the show. Sitting Bull did little more than sit impassively on horseback while being introduced to crowds. He was routinely booed and insulted wherever the show went, except in Canada, where he was cheered. However, Sitting Bull got a bit of his own back. He not only was paid quite well—fifty dollars a week plus a signing bonus of $125—but he also signed autographs and sold photos of himself, keeping the proceeds. Moreover, he got Cody to guarantee him all the oyster stew he could eat.

Famed Native American Chief Geronimo toured with Cody's Wild West show. Chiefs such as Geronimo and Sitting Bull were well known throughout the country.

Sitting Bull got along well with most of the rest of the cast. He was especially fond of Annie Oakley, whom he called "Little Sure Shot." His relationship with Cody, however, was complicated. On the one hand, Cody once called him a "peevish Indian" who "refused to talk English, even if he could." [70] On the other, Cody gave Sitting Bull a trick horse and a hat when he left the show, and Sitting Bull carried fond memories of Cody afterwards: "My friend Long Hair gave me this hat," he told a relative who tried to put it on once. "I value it very highly, for the hand that placed it on my head had a friendly feeling for me." [71]

Unfortunately, Sitting Bull did not live long after leaving Cody's company. In 1890, he was shot and killed during a protest near the Standing Rock Reservation. Some government officials blamed his involvement in Wild West shows. They said the shows had given Sitting Bull a sense of "inordinate pride" [72] which led him to urge rebellion against the policies of the Indian agents.

Black Elk was another Wild West Indian whose name is recognized today. His story, however, is quite different from Sitting Bull's. Black Elk became famous as a holy man and healer, not a military leader, and he rose to prominence after appearing in a show, not before. His autobiography, *Black Elk Speaks*, was first published in 1932 and remains popular today. His account of being an "ordinary" show Indian provides an excellent picture of what touring was like for Native Americans.

As a young man, Black Elk joined Cody's show for the adventure and sailed for Europe. The trip across the ocean was sheer misery. Not used to large ships and ocean swells, Black Elk and the other Indians aboard were seriously affected by the ship's motion. Many of the Indians, he remembered years later, were feeling so sick, that they began to sing their death songs. When evening came, a big wind was roaring and the water thundered. . . . The floor tipped in every direction, and this got worse and worse, so that we rolled from one side to the other and could not sleep. [73]

Once in England, things improved—for a while. Black Elk danced for Queen Victoria, whom he described as "little but fat." [74] Then he and several other Indians accidentally got separated from the group in Manchester, England, when Cody was about to leave for America again. Black Elk made his way to London, joined Mexican Joe's Wild West, and toured

Sitting Bull and Buffalo Bill pose for a photograph. Because he was considered responsible for George Armstrong Custer's death, Sitting Bull was often booed and hissed when he performed in Cody's show.

Germany and France with him. Eventually he ran into Cody again in France. Cody offered Black Elk his old job back, but Black Elk refused; he wanted instead to go home. Cody gave him ninety dollars and bought him a ticket to the U.S. "I was sick part of the time," Black Elk remembered about the voyage back, "but I was not sad, because I was going home."[75]

"Our People Will Wonder at These Things"

The responses of Wild West Indians when they returned home varied. Sitting Bull came home awed by the numbers of white people he had seen on tour. He said,

> The White people are so many that if every Indian in the West killed one every step they took, the dead would not be missed among you. I go back and tell my people what I have seen. They will never go on the warpath again.[76]

But Sitting Bull also returned disgusted by the poverty, the pace of life, and the confusion of white society. "The tipi is a better place," he said, explaining his decision not to sign on with Cody for another season. "I am sick of the houses and the noises and the multitude of men."[77]

Many other Indians, such as American Horse, also came back from their travels world-weary and convinced that their own culture was best. But some had a different spin. Red Shirt said,

> I started from my lodge two moons ago knowing nothing, and had I remained on the Indian Reservations, I should have been as a blind man. Now I can see a new dawn. [I have seen] the great houses [that

is, ships] which cross the mighty waters, the great villages which have no end where the pale faces swarm like insects in the summer sun. . . . Our people will wonder at these things when we return to the Indian Reservation and tell them what we have seen.[78]

The Indian agents varied, too, in their views of what Wild West shows did to Indians. Some saw jaded, disrespectful Indians returning, men and women who now wanted what they could not have and who had been corrupted along the tour. "Traveling with a show," said one agent who had seen several of his charges leave the reservation and then return, "only encourages an Indian in his already strong habits of idleness and vice."[79] Others, however, viewed things differently. An Arizona agent reported that returning Indians had "a tendency to enlighten those who have remained at home."[80] Another agreed. "For morals and good behavior," he wrote Cody, the Indians who traveled with Cody's show "have done a great deal better while away with you than their comrades who remained here have done."[81]

Treatment

In part, the government was reluctant to allow Wild West shows to hire Indians because of a few cases in which Indians had been poorly fed, unpaid, or left stranded in cities far from their homes. In one notable case from 1886, a group of nineteen Indians was stranded in Tennessee when a promoter closed his show and ran off. Several Indians died, mostly of disease, while shows were touring Europe, leading to charges that they were not being properly taken care of. Cody created a stir when he sent some sick Indians home from England one year. One eventually died of tuberculosis, which led to an investigation of the treatment of Indians by Wild West shows in general and by Cody's show in particular.

Certainly, Indians often were not treated fairly. The Miller Brothers contracted with a man named W. H. Barten to provide Indians for their shows. Barten took money off the Indians' salaries as a fee, and then insisted on handling the Indians' remaining finances as well, with the connivance of the Millers. A man named Bear Shield, for instance, signed on for five dollars a week, of which four went directly to Barten. Moreover, once a Native American joined a show, it was often hard for him to get out. Barten and the Millers gave the Indians credit to buy costumes, food, and the like, which gave them leverage in negotiations. They insisted that all debts be paid before an Indian left the show, especially if he was planning to join someone else's company. "By going away from the 101," Barten told Bear Runs in the Woods, "you would place yourself liable to arrest for getting of [from] me goods under false pretenses."[82]

Other shows had problems, too. Luther Standing Bear, the Sioux interpreter on one of Cody's European tours, liked and admired Cody and the other show personnel. Yet he remembered several times when the Indians were patronized or mistreated. "You always give [the Indians] the wild horses to ride," he complained to the show's chief cowboy once.

So-called Spies from Serbia

In 1914, nine Oglala Sioux Indians were performing in Germany with Colonel Cummins's Wild West when the First World War broke out. Tensions between European countries were high, and the German authorities were deeply concerned about any foreigners who happened to be in their midst. The Oglalas worried them particularly.

While the Oglalas and their interpreter, Bill Arthur, insisted that they were genuine Native Americans, the German government was less certain. The Oglalas did not dress offstage as they did while performing. Moreover, some of the members of the group had cut their hair short and wore wigs in the arena. They did not look like stereotypical Indians, still less like the Indians they portrayed during the Wild West show. To make matters worse, the Indians lacked valid papers proving who they were. Taking all this into account, the German police decided the Indians were not Indians after all.

Instead, the police determined, they were clearly spies from Serbia, an Eastern European country which opposed Germany during the war. All nine men were arrested and put in jail.

Arthur appealed immediately to H. H. Morgan, American consul general in Hamburg, who got the men temporarily released so they could stand trial. But Arthur and Morgan were not confident that they would be able to prove the truth. Instead, they smuggled the Indians into Denmark. They were then taken to Norway, Holland, and England before finally returning home. Years later, as quoted in L. C. Moses' book, *Wild West Shows and the Image of the American Indian*, Morgan wrote to Arthur and reminded him about "the good old times in Hamburg when the Germans tried to shoot the feathers off the aggregation of Indians which you had with you."

Most Native Americans were well treated in the traveling Wild West shows. In this photograph, Native Americans seem to be contentedly joking with one another.

"Then, when they have the horse nicely broken, you give it to a cowboy."[83] On another occasion, Indians were served leftovers for lunch while other cast members were given something fresh. Cody agreed with Standing Bear that this was unfair. "My Indians are the principal feature of this show," Cody told the manager of the cook tent, "and they are the one people I will not allow to be misused or neglected."[84]

But most Wild West Indians seem to have been treated reasonably well. Very little evidence of mistreatment turned up during the investigation of Cody's show. Those interviewed by authorities had few complaints; to a man they said they had been dealt with humanely. In Berlin, the American consul general wrote:

We take great pleasure in stating that we visited the Buffalo Bill Wild West show in Berlin, and have seen the Indians both in their tents and during the performance. They are certainly the best looking and apparently the best fed Indians we have ever seen.[85]

Nor was Cody's show alone. The American Wild West Company hired a Sioux interpreter, Frank Goings, who wrote to the Pine Ridge reservation's agent every week. "Indians all well and fat as Pigs," he wrote once. "They get all they can eat and more too."[86]

Of course, Native Americans were not treated precisely as the white performers were. They were not paid as well. They were more likely to be exploited in other ways. Unlike the whites, they generally did not speak English, were not part of the culture of the cities where they traveled, and stood out everywhere they went. There is also no question that the use of Indians in shows encouraged damaging stereotypes about Indians. While most Wild West shows did play up the horsemanship, the artistry, and the courage of the Native Americans, they rarely presented the Indians as whole people. Instead, they portrayed Indians as half-naked, ignorant, and bloodthirsty savages whose main claim to fame was in having gotten in the way of progress.

Nevertheless, the total picture of Indian involvement in Wild West shows is complicated. Wild West shows were a broadening experience for many Indians. They gave Native American men and women a chance to see the world beyond their reservations and to meet people of many different backgrounds. "My father liked to travel and went with Cody every chance he got,"[87] remembered a Sioux man. "Before he died, he said he had visited every European country except Portugal." While not every Wild West Indian signed up for multiple tours, many did—and of those who chose not to, few seem to have resented the time they spent on tour. The recollections and interviews of Indians who joined Wild West shows indicate that many, perhaps most, Indian participants enjoyed the work and the opportunities it gave them.

Indians made enormous contributions to Wild West shows. It would have been possible to have put white actors in the roles of Indians, but promoters mainly rejected this option. Indians provided realism and a sense of extra excitement. Historians may continue to argue about the effect of Wild West shows on the stereotypes Americans hold about Indians today. Wild West shows could have gone on without Indians, but they would have been different indeed—and less effective as well.

5 On the Move

Travel was a constant for nearly every Wild West show. Except for a few long-term stands in big cities such as Chicago, New York, or London, Wild West companies moved at least once or twice a week, often once a day. The ever-changing schedule irritated some performers and delighted others. It required remarkable precision, both in arranging routes and in preparing the show to be moved. Being part of a Wild West show meant travel. It is difficult to imagine the Wild West without movement.

The miles covered could be enormous. In 1896, Cody's show spent four solid weeks at Madison Square Garden in New York City. Nevertheless, the show still racked up 10,787 miles during the remaining months of the season. The year before, Cody had played 131 different towns in 190 days. Even when mileage was not especially great, packing up and moving on every day grew arduous. Besides being costly and time-consuming, travel could be risky. Bad weather, transportation problems, poor advertising, and economic depression could cause a show to lose money in a hurry. Still, most promoters had little choice. Staying in one location for a length of time was simply not feasible. Even in the biggest cities, crowds eventually dried up.

Fortunately, while touring was expensive, there was the potential to make quite a bit of money in a short time. During the period before movies, radio, and television, outdoor entertainments were very popular. With poor roads and little leisure time, people stayed close to home for the entertainments they did attend. As a result, a one-day stand, even in a small town, could fill the arena and bring in more than enough money to get the show safely to its next destination.

Most shows traveled primarily by train. Railroads were the fastest means of transportation in a time of dirt and gravel roads and no automobiles or trucks. They had the added advantage of going almost everywhere. Between 1880 and 1920 virtually every American town of any consequence had its own railroad station and at least one set of tracks. Train travel was therefore efficient as well as fast.

However, companies did occasionally use other means. Those who went to Europe, of course, traveled on ships. And a few Wild West shows moved up and down the rivers of America on steamboats, playing mostly at towns along the Ohio, Mississippi, and Tennessee Rivers. The most successful shows not only presented good entertainment, they also knew how to move from one place to another with a minimum of time and expense.

Advance Men

In some ways, the most important employees of a Wild West show were not performers at all. Rather, they were the so-called "advance men." Nearly every show, no matter how small, had at least one or two, even if they doubled in performing, administration, or support roles. The advance men's duties were

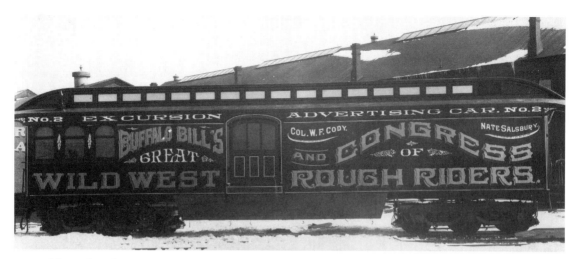

One of the railroad cars that carried Cody's Wild West show. Scheduling the show's appearances throughout the country to avoid other Wild West shows and to keep traveling to a minimum was a daunting task.

many; they were also vital to the success of their companies.

Their work began during the winter, when they would work with other administrators and sketch out a rough route map for the upcoming season. Picking towns and dates was complicated. First, of course, advance men had to try to keep travel to a minimum. Constant touring was both hard on the performers and prohibitively expensive. Freight costs rose by the mile, and when a large show used dozens of railroad cars to move it along, every mile mattered. It made no sense, geographically, to go from Chicago to San Francisco and then back to Kansas City, and the question of minimizing travel was foremost in the planners' minds.

However, geography could not be the only consideration. Schedulers also had to take into account weather patterns, current events, and local customs. There was no value in being in a town during the rainy season, for instance, or playing in a farming community at harvest time. Nor could shows make money in areas affected by high unemployment, gen-

eral strikes, or depression. Similarly, many shows tried to avoid small towns where they had played the year before. Unless they had gotten extraordinarily large and enthusiastic crowds, most show schedulers preferred to route their companies elsewhere for a year or two. Extra miles were worth it to avoid performing in places where audiences were not likely to attend.

Scheduling really became an art form, however, in determining a route that would avoid other circuses and Wild West shows. In most cases, there was no point in arriving in a town just behind another entertainment. The first show would have already taken the local people's money. On the other hand, it was not always in the interest of a small show to come to town just before a more famous large one did. Given that case, townspeople often saved their cash for the second one. Advance men eagerly scanned their rivals' schedules to see where they might conflict with their own.

Once the season began, the advance man's job was to drum up business and make final arrangements for the show. Typically, he would travel the show's scheduled route, arriving in each town a week or ten days before the rest of the troupe. He was responsible for making sure that everything was in order for the performance—that sites were available, that fees had been paid, and that the town was sufficiently interested in the show. To that end he also spent time and money on advertising. If a community seemed uninterested in the show; if a drought, tornado, or massive layoff had crippled the economy; or if a competitor had just arrived in town, then the advance man would make a change in plans and route the show elsewhere.

Advertising

Posters were the most common way of advertising a show. Many Wild West companies produced brilliant posters, usually in full color. Advance men traveled with dozens of these posters in different sizes. The smallest in common use were twenty-eight by forty-two inches. The largest were twenty-four times as big and were printed in six different sections. The advance crews used brushes with handles ten feet long to apply paste to blank walls, fences, windows, or any other available surface. Then they stuck the poster in place and smoothed out any wrinkles.

The posters were not intended to be permanent, and most were soon destroyed by weather; they only needed to last till the show itself arrived. Nevertheless, many of the posters were quite beautiful. They often included elaborate paintings of scenes and performers from the show. A 101 Ranch poster, for instance, showed a chariot race with horses thundering in every direction, dust billowing from behind the riders. A poster from Tiger Bill's Wild West illustrated a fight between Indians and U.S. soldiers, complete with blood, bucking horses, buildings on fire, and puffs of smoke from gunfire. Most posters were specific to individual shows and sometimes even individual performances, but a few smaller shows relied on printing companies that sold stock Wild West posters. The printers only had to add the show's name at the bottom.

Larger shows often ordered thousands of posters at a time, and advance agents used them all. Vacant houses were plastered with signs in a matter of minutes. Advance men gave farmers tickets to the show in exchange for barn space. Farmers often were just as happy to have the posters covering chinks in the barn walls. Advance men tacked posters onto trees and glued them on public buildings. By whatever means necessary, the community was covered. "Every billboard from one end of town to the other was plastered

Many of the posters that advertised an upcoming visit of a Wild West show were quite intricately painted.

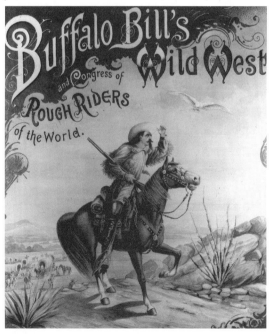

with billings," an observer remarked about an Ohio town, "and the business places along Main Street had the bills in their windows."[88]

Billing Wars and Bankruptcy

Advance agents from different shows sometimes crossed paths, with unfortunate results. "Billing wars," where one show attempted to out-advertise another, were common. At times these threatened to put companies out of business. Cody's Wild West was especially good at driving his competitors into bankruptcy with this method. Doc Carver, he remembered with satisfaction in 1905, had

> jumped in ahead of me in 1885. And tryed to take my route away from me. Well I followed right behind him. And billed and advertised the same towns he did. And kept it up until I broke him.[89]

Cody tried the same trick at least twice more, as well. In one instance when Pawnee Bill Lillie reached a town first, Cody had his advance agents put up posters that advised "Wait for the Big Show! Buffalo Bill Is Coming."[90] Cody also destroyed a competitor's show in Europe, forcing the founder of the show to leave England just ahead of his creditors.

Another way to hurt a competitor was to destroy or cover over his posters. Putting a poster on top of an opponent's poster was not ethical but was nevertheless often done. In some cases a poster might be covered and recovered four or five times. At least one crew, having run out of their own posters, pasted blank newspaper over the posters belonging to a rival. Tearing down a poster was harder, but advance men did it when they felt it was necessary. With competitive feelings so high,

tempers occasionally flared. A few advance men were seriously hurt in fights.

Besides posters, Wild West companies used handbills, newspaper advertisements, and booklets to advertise their upcoming attractions. Advance agents either passed out handbills and booklets themselves or hired children to do the job for them. Still, posters were the primary way of letting people know that the show was soon to arrive. Once everything was in order, the agents would move on to the next stop along the route and begin the

Annie Oakley's stunts are advertised in the background of this poster. Posters were the main way to advertise an upcoming show, and competitors would often try to eliminate one another's billings.

BUFFALO BILL'S WILD WEST.
CONGRESS, ROUGH RIDERS OF THE WORLD.

MISS ANNIE OAKLEY,
THE PEERLESS LADY WING-SHOT.

In a reenactment, trained horses and their riders simulate a battle between cowboys and Native Americans called "defending the wagon train." Often performed on little more than vacant lots, shows brought their own seating and grandstands with them.

process all over again. Many shows, though not all, used special railroad cars for their advance crews. At least one newspaper found these worth describing in some detail:

> At one end is the office of the car manager; at the other a boiler is convenient for the purpose of making paste, should the show at anytime go to a small country place where billposters and paste are alike unknown. Between the office and the boiler in the car there are large lockers where hundreds of different kinds of posters are systematically arranged. Above these are tables where the slips giving the name of the city and the date of the exposition's visit are attached. Above the tables, again, are the sleeping bunks.[91]

The advance man, many observers noted, could either make a show or break it. With a well-planned schedule and plenty of prior warning to towns and cities, a Wild West company could draw good crowds and make enough money to stay on the road another year. Poor planning and insufficient advertising, though, drove several shows into bankruptcy. When shows folded, too, advance men were often blamed. An observer wrote angrily,

> Without question, the advance man broke the 101 Ranch show during the 1931 season. He would send the show on a 250 mile jump one night (freight $900) and the next night 250 miles back to within 50 miles of where the show had previously been. He would route the show into towns where the police and fireman were having benefit rodeos or into towns where most of the population was out on strike from the mills and factories. Colonel [Zack] Miller was informed of the deplorable situation but was too busy at the ranch . . . to pay much attention and the needless expense and loss in ticket receipts continued.[92]

1931 was indeed the show's last year.

"A Very Extraordinary & Interesting Sight"

Wild West shows were, in some ways, even more successful and popular in Europe than in America. Many large shows, and several small ones, toured England or the European continent at least once. Cody's show played twice for England's Queen Victoria, the first time on May 11, 1887. The queen recorded her impressions of the show in her journal, as quoted in Joseph Rosa's *Buffalo Bill and His Wild West*:

"[We went] to Earl's Court, where we saw a very extraordinary & interesting sight, a performance of 'Buffalo Bill's Wild West.' We sat in a box in a large semi circle. It is an amphitheater with a large open space, all the seats being under cover. All of the different people, wild, painted Red Indians from America on their wild bare backed horses, of different tribes,—cow boys, Mexicans, &c., all came tearing round at full speed, shrieking & screaming, which had the weirdest effect. An attack on a coach & on a ranch, with an immense deal of firing, was most exciting, so was the buffalo hunt, & the bucking ponies, that were almost impossible to sit. The cow boys, are fine looking people, but the painted Indians, with their feathers, & wild dress (very little of it) were rather alarming looking, & they had cruel faces. A young girl, who went through the 'haute ecole,' [an equestrian demonstration] certainly sat the most marvellous plunges beautifully, sitting quite erect, & being completely master of her horse. There were 2 other girls, who shot with an unvarying aim at glass balls. Col. Cody 'Buffalo Bill' as he is called, from having killed 3000 buffaloes, with his own hand, is a splendid man, handsome, & gentlemanlike in manner. He has had many encounters & hand to hand fights with the Red Indians. Their War Dance, to a wild drum & pipe, was quite fearful, with all their contorsions & shrieks, & they came so close. 'Red Shirt' the Chief of the Sioux tribe, was presented to me & so were the squaws, with their papooses (children) who shook hands with me."

Performance Sites

As a rule, Wild West shows performed outdoors. Nearly all indoor arenas of the time were too small to accommodate anything but a scaled-down show. The few that were large enough were expensive to rent and often had other drawbacks, including very little space outside the arena for demonstrations and setting up equipment. Once in a while a show might be booked into a fairgrounds, a racetrack, or a baseball field that already had permanent seating, but this seems to have been the exception rather than the rule. More often, shows played on vacant lots.

But not just any lot would do. A show the size of Cody's spread out over several acres of land once it arrived at its destination. The 101 Ranch Wild West's arena alone measured almost a quarter of a million square feet; the tents, wagons, walkways, and stables that made up the grounds were larger still. Not only did the site have to be big, it also had to be relatively flat, easily accessible to the people of the town, and as close as possible to a railroad line if the show traveled by train. Some of these requirements were not possible to meet, which meant more work for the crew, cramped quarters for the performers, lower attendance, or all three.

Since large Wild West shows rarely performed where there was already seating, the amount of equipment the shows needed was staggering. Most shows carried their own grandstands, their own tents, their own canvas coverings, and their own lighting equipment, not to mention livestock, costumes, and set pieces. The larger the show, the more complicated the touring. In 1898, for instance, more than 450 people traveled with Cody's show. The show's train included thirty-nine different cars, not counting engine, coal car, and caboose. Eight cars were designated as sleeping coaches for performers, crew, and families. Fifteen more were intended for the animals, and the rest carried baggage, wagons, and set pieces such as the stagecoach, saddles, water tanks, and other pieces of essential equipment.

The list of equipment was similar to that of a circus, but there was one important difference. It was not practical for Wild West shows to perform with a circus-style big top. As one participant put it, "The type of performance with its many shooting events, which would have ruined an overhead canvas, precluded its being given in the usual circus tents."[93] Nevertheless, most large shows did set up canvas covers for the grandstand. If performers got wet or baked in the hot sun, the audience could still sit in relative comfort.

Even without a canvas big top, however, the Wild West show carried an astonishing amount of equipment. The Cody Wild West route book of 1896 listed some of the necessary materials. To construct an enclosed arena, crew members set up what one eyewitness described as "large heavy canvas for a side wall . . . 10 to 12 feet in height."[94] That wall used up five thousand yards of canvas. Covering the grandstand required seven thousand more. Setting up all the tents used over a thousand stakes, each of which had to be put in exactly the right spot—day after day

after day. Cody's show carried so much lighting equipment as it traveled that one historian has called it "the largest private electrical plant in existence at the time."[95] The show also used twenty *miles* of rope.

Set Up and Strike

Most large shows traveled with a team of "roustabouts," or men whose job was to set up the show each time it arrived in a new place. Cody's show carried as many as seventy-two of these men, though the number varied from year to year. The work was heavy, but the men who did it followed strict systems designed to make it as easy and swift as possible. In general, the first piece to be put up was the canvas tent that covered the grandstand. Once this was in place, the team assembled the grandstand itself according to careful measurements and drawings. The process was complicated, involving jobs such as "stringer-setter," "toe leveler," and "block boy."[96]

While the arena was being constructed, other members of the crew handled different chores. Some pounded in stakes to anchor the various tents, including the cooking tent, the blacksmith's tent, livestock tents, and tents where performers slept, if the show was to stay overnight. Others got the ticket wagon ready for the evening's show, unloaded and organized props, or moved horses and buffalo from the train to their portable stables.

Then, in the evening, once the performances were over, the roustabouts had to strike the show, or undo the whole job. Courtney Ryley Cooper, who spent time with Cody's company, described a typical scene as the show was being picked up:

Tired, struggling horses floundered through the mud as they hauled the

Lights!

No piece of equipment was more important to a Wild West show than the electric lights, and Wild West shows traveled with plenty of them. Lights made it possible to perform after dark. While lights would not adequately illuminate large areas such as baseball fields until well into the twentieth century, it was common for Wild West shows to use them in their arenas many years earlier. During the 1890s, for instance, Cody's Wild West trained twenty-four carbon arc lights into the arena for evening performances, though no more than twelve at a time could actually be turned on. The 101 Ranch boasted that its lights were powerful enough to help audiences pick out a pin anywhere in the arena. Shows also illuminated the grandstand to help people get in and out of their seats and read the program; for this purpose

Cody's show set up four hundred incandescent lamps.

Other lights were necessary as well. Cody traveled with three enormous searchlights. Wild West shows used these lights to pick out star performers, to heighten dramatic tension, and to follow the moving targets during the sharpshooting acts. The marksmen and women had to see what they were aiming at, and even more important, the audience had to see whether or not the target was hit. The tents and grounds were lit up at night, too, with lights similar to those set in the grandstand and arenas. Portable generators provided the power. The equipment itself must surely have taken a great deal of space on the trains, and Cody had to employ eleven workers simply to run and set up the electric lights.

The portable generators that provided the lighting for Cody's Wild West show.

Men set up the huge tent for the performance of the Wild West show. The tent was the first thing to be set up.

wagons to the loading runs for their journey to the next town. Here and there, shadowy, vague, in the misty light, the "pick-up" crew moved about the lot; there is always extra caution on a rainy night that every item of paraphernalia be catalogued, every movement checked, to guard against valuable perquisites being left behind.[97]

Especially in later years, when it was possible and common to use artificial light, striking the show might not begin until close to midnight. Following similar routines to the morning's work, though mainly in reverse, the workers put away the canvas, disassembled the grandstand, packed up props, costumes, and livestock, and loaded everything aboard the train again. Everything had its proper place, and the placement had its own logic. What was needed first the next day was loaded into the train cars last; what would not be needed until later was loaded in first, or might even be placed on a separate train due to arrive later the following day.

The life of a roustabout was a hard one. Workdays of sixteen hours, six days a week, were common. When shows chose to perform far from from the railroad tracks, the roustabouts suffered more than anyone. In those circumstances, all equipment and animals had to be transported by wagon from the trains to the grounds and then returned the same way; this could easily tack on an extra few hours to an already long workday. At best, the work was rough and occasionally backbreaking. At worst, roustabouts struggled with their jobs in the rain, in cold, in almost complete darkness, all too often in the mud, and sleep was a precious commodity.

Not surprisingly, the roustabouts sometimes worked too quickly. According to Cody's 1896 route book, the crews once began to take down the arena canvas even before the band had finished playing the evening's final concert. In another case, a

William Cody, Johnnie Baker, and John Burke stand in front of the Deadwood Stagecoach. When a Wild West show traveled overseas, it was especially difficult and expensive to transport props such as the stagecoach and livestock.

young, inexperienced roustabout could not find two important boards while packing up. With the train ready to leave for the next town, he grabbed two he could find near the lot and tossed them onto the train. The next morning a cast member discovered that one of the boards bore the inscription "Here rests in peace the remains of Joshua Pepper."[98] Fortunately, the grave marker was wrapped up and sent back to the town where it had been found.

If loading a train was difficult, loading a show onto a ship was practically impossible. Cody rented a steamship called the *State of Nebraska* to bring his show to England in 1887. Most of the larger pieces of equipment, such as the stagecoach, had to be hauled over the side of the ship. So did many of the animals. According to most witnesses, the horses

and the deer struggled and panicked while being loaded on. The buffalo, on the other hand,

> went over without a murmur, though almost scared to death. The people who watched the transfer from the shore made the interesting discovery that a horned buffalo being yanked over the ship's side in a sling, hanging up by the middle with head and heels together, is a much more comical sight than anything in the show itself, and they laughed until their sides ached, though the buffalo didn't seem to find it amusing.[99]

Dangers of Touring

While travel itself was not usually dangerous, there were several disasters involving touring

Wild West shows. The first of these occurred in the Mississippi River during the winter of 1884–85, while Cody was on his way to New Orleans by steamboat. At Rodney Island, Mississippi, the boat collided with another boat and sank. No one was hurt. The horses were saved, too, but most of the show's props, sets, and costumes sank and were lost or ruined.

According to legend, Cody wired Nate Salsbury, who was performing with another group in Denver that night. "Outfit at bottom of river," Cody wrote; "what do you advise?"[100] Salsbury received the telegram just as he was about to go onstage. He had his band leader repeat a musical interlude to give him time to think. Then he cabled Cody back with the message "Go to New Orleans, reorganize, and open on your date."[101] Cody salvaged the Deadwood stagecoach, bought new equipment, and did exactly what Salsbury suggested.

Travel by ship across the Atlantic similarly did not cause many injuries, but did make many Wild West performers and crew members extremely seasick. While Indian actors, such as Black Elk, seem to have been especially susceptible to motion sickness, whites often were laid low for most of the trip as well. After arriving safely in England aboard the *State of Nebraska*, Cody admitted that he had been "sick as a cow with a hollow horn"[102] throughout the ocean voyage. Still, the *State of Nebraska* was lucky to escape serious damage. During a violent storm, the ship's propeller had broken. It took two days to make the necessary

Learning from the Wild West

The First World War broke out twenty-five years after Annie Oakley toured Europe with Buffalo Bill's Wild West. Yet that show played a part in the war—a part which Oakley, for one, regretted years afterwards. Here she is quoted in Courtney Ryley Cooper's *Annie Oakley: Woman at Arms*:

"We saw the Kaiser [German emperor Wilhelm] five or six times during our stay in Germany. His thoughts were bent upon military efficiency to a degree almost inconceivable to us at the time. He did not care about the show as an exhibition, but centred his entire interest upon the mechanical aspect of it and the lessons which could be learned from us for use in the handling of his military.

We never moved without at least forty officers of the Prussian Guard standing all about with notebooks, taking down every detail of the performance. They made minute notes of how we pitched camp—the exact number of men needed, every man's position, how long it took, how we boarded the trains and packed the horses and broke camp; every rope and bundle and kit was inspected and mapped.

But most of all, they took interest in our kitchen. The travelling ranges were inspected and enumerated in those endless note-books. The chefs were interviewed. The methods of storing food, of preparing it, of having necessities ready for use at a minute's notice, all these things were jotted down. Naturally we were curious as to why they were doing all this. . . . But we had no idea, of course, that the world was to listen, mouth open, twenty-five years later, to the stories of the marvellous travelling kitchens of the Teuton Army, serving meals piping hot on the road to Brussels—an idea gained from the Buffalo Bill Wild West show when we toured Germany!"

repairs, during which time the ship had drifted more than two hundred miles off course.

Train travel, however, was not merely inconvenient. It could be deadly. On a trip from Charlotte, North Carolina, to Danville, Virginia, in 1901, Cody's train collided with a freight train. One hundred and ten horses were killed. While no person died, Annie Oakley was seriously injured in the crash. It took her many years to recover, and she never appeared with Cody's show again. An even more serious crash took place three years later outside Maywood, Illinois, on a train bringing Wild West show Sioux to New York to board a ship for Europe. Luther Standing Bear barely survived, and wrote about the wreck in his autobiography:

> We were rounding a curve, when suddenly I saw a train behind us coming at lightning speed. Then came a terrific crash. There was not even time to cry out. When I opened my eyes again, the seats were piled up on top of us and the steam and smoke from the engine were pouring in on us in great clouds. My legs were pinned down, and I was perfectly helpless. The moaning of the injured and the screams of many of the white people in the car were terrible. Blood was everywhere.[103]

Three died in the crash; twenty-seven others were badly hurt, including Standing Bear.

Life in a Wild West show would no doubt have been easier if the shows had done less traveling. Some tried. Cody's show did wonderful business at least twice in New York City. The 101 Ranch show was successful for a time performing at home in Oklahoma. Cody's Wild West also played to thousands of fans during the Columbian Exposition of 1893 in Chicago. Certainly there were many advantages to staying in one place: performers had better accommodations, fewer crew members were required, scenery could be more elaborate, advertising and logistics were far simpler. But in the end, staying in one place was not usually lucrative.

And in the end, too, traveling contributed to the success of Wild West shows. The excitement created by the arrival of an outfit in a town, no matter how small the show or how small the town, was remarkable. Parades, billposting, and the daily setup and strike added to the romance of the Wild West show for many audience members. Moreover, the success of Wild West shows was directly based on their traveling. Had they stayed in just a few large cities, they could never have become popular all across the country as they ultimately did.

Daily Life

There were many differences among Wild West shows, and many more differences among Wild West performers. The experience of a show employee varied depending on whether the employee was a man or a woman; a performer or a roustabout; a headliner or an ordinary cowboy; a Native American or a Cossack. Experiences varied, too, according to the size of the show, the financial stability of its owners, and whether the show traveled extensively or played longer stands. Nevertheless, there were several constants that affected nearly everyone affiliated with any Wild West show. Despite the differences, daily life for most Wild West employees tended to follow very similar patterns.

Perhaps the most obvious of these was organization. Wild West shows, especially those that toured, ran on tight, rigorous schedules. Performers and support personnel had assigned bunks on trains, specific mealtimes, designated dressing rooms, and restrictions on what they could carry with them while traveling. Shows often attempted, with more or less success, to regulate their employees' hours off as well. Many of the restrictions seem excessive today, but management saw them as necessary to ensure the smooth running of the show.

A second constant was boredom. This affected performers in particular. Except for the orator and perhaps a few others, most Wild West actors were off stage for much of the performance—in some cases nearly all. Most shows did not encourage their employees to watch from the wings or from the grandstand. Practicing was difficult when the show was going on, and many performers did not need much practice anyway, since they so often performed two shows a day. This led to a lot of dull stretches, which performers had to find a way to fill.

And yet a third constant was travel. Even when shows settled in for a three- or four-month run in the same spot, performers and

Sightseeing

The Indians who traveled with Wild West shows were particularly interested in the sights of foreign countries. Native Americans in the employ of one show or another danced in front of Italy's Mount Vesuvius. They also visited Pope Leo XIII in the Vatican, Heidelberg Castle in Germany, the battlefield of Waterloo, the canals and gondolas of Venice, and many other important sites. Interested though the Indians were, however, they never forgot their homeland and their ancestry. In Spain, Major John Burke showed off a statue of Christopher Columbus. "There," he said, as quoted in Carolyn Foreman's book, *Indians Abroad*, "stands our advance agent, four hundred years ahead of us." One unidentified Wild West show Indian, who spoke good English, was quick with his retort: "It was a damned bad [day] for us when he discovered America."

most crew members were not truly "home." At best, they were living in a home away from home—in tents scattered around the arena, in the show train, or in cheap hotels and rooming houses. But then, so were performers who traveled on a daily basis. Whether they were in Nebraska, Pennsylvania, or Georgia, they also returned to the same sleeping car or tent every night. Neither was a very stable existence, and virtually all Wild West performers were affected by being away from family, friends, and home.

Multicultural Casts

Living in a Wild West show was a communal experience. There was little privacy and little time to be alone. Except for a handful of stars, every cast and crew member doubled or tripled up when it came to sleeping, dressing, and eating. Since so much was shared, getting along with other people was a high priority. Those who had trouble cooperating usually left the show before long, either by their own choice or by the decision of management. And getting along was especially important because of the multicultural nature of Wild West shows.

America around the turn of the century was a land of immigrants. Still, there was not much mixing between groups. Native Americans lived on reservations, for the most part. Certain white ethnic groups tended to settle in the same neighborhoods, or sometimes even in entire towns and counties. As late as the First World War, visitors to some American communities were better off knowing

"A Great Day for Them to Come Back"

Very little is known about the final burial sites of the Wild West performers who died and were buried in England. However, the graves of two Native American performers were the subject of newspaper reports in 1997.

Long Wolf, a Lakota Sioux leader, died of pneumonia in the summer of 1892 at the age of 59. His body was buried in a wooden casket in a London cemetery, along with the remains of White Star, a 17-month-old Sioux girl who had died after a fall from a horse. There the two bodies lay for about a century. Then an English woman who knew the story and the location of the grave tracked down Long Wolf's relatives in the United States and suggested that they bring the bodies back home for reburial.

Long Wolf's descendants did. In September 1997, Long Wolf and White Star were buried again on a hillside in South Dakota. The original casket had long since fallen apart, so a replica was used instead. The ceremony was a traditional Sioux one, mixed with Christian gospel music. Participants agreed that the reburial was appropriate. "[England is] not our home," said Wilmer Mesteth, quoted in the Spokane *Spokesman-Review* of September 29, 1997, who presided at the service. "It's so different." Moreover, the reburial celebrated the lives of Long Wolf and White Star—and by extension the lives of all Indians who performed in the shows. "Many went to Europe to perform," said one observer. "Many came back. But Long Wolf and White Star did not. This is a great day for them to come back."

German, Italian, or Czech than English. And African Americans, of course, were often segregated by law from the white majority.

Wild West shows, however, were different. Few areas of American society were as well integrated culturally as these shows. Each non-English-speaking group had its own interpreter, like the Sioux's Luther Standing Bear. These interpreters translated for those who could not speak English and also acted as advocates, making sure that their charges' rights were respected. While some cast members relied on the interpreters for everything, never attempting to learn any English, this was not true of all performers. Charles Griffin, who traveled with the show, wrote:

> Col. Cody's exhibition is unique in many ways, and might justly be termed a polyglot school, no less than twelve distinct languages being spoken in the camp, viz.: Japanese, Russian, French, Arabic, Greek, Hungarian, German, Italian, Spanish, Holland, Flemish, Chinese, Sioux, and English. Being in such close contact every day, we were bound to get some idea of each other's tongue, and all acquire a fair idea of English.[104]

Of course, cultural differences sometimes did keep people apart. In at least some shows Indians had a different dining tent from white performers. Cody hired no black performers until 1894, and few thereafter. However, in general the closeness to other people seems to have encouraged separate groups to make friends—and sometimes more. According to Pawnee Bill Lillie:

> There were always many an affecting scene at the closing of our show. I have seen a big Indian chief holding the hand of a Russian Cossack, or perhaps an Arab dancing girl, each looking the other straight in the eye with an expression of regret, neither being able to even say good-bye in a language common to both.

> Many peculiar and strange attachments, even unions, were made. Our show physician was a graduate of one of our best medical colleges and from one of the finest families of Virginia. . . . He married the prettiest little Russian dancing girl, who could not speak a word of English.[105]

Marriages like these were not uncommon. Racial boundaries were even crossed, as in Cody's show, where an Englishwoman and an Indian fell in love and married. "Generally," Pawnee Bill asserted, "a marriage with the show meant the exit of the pair from show life forever."[106]

While that may have been true for couples who met and fell in love while performing, shows often hired married couples. Indian men were encouraged to bring their wives, and as time went on, white performers were also allowed to do so. Some wives came as part of a husband-and-wife team, each hired on his or her merits as a performer. Others simply accompanied their husbands. They often were asked to appear in crowd scenes or as performers in the pre-show events and demonstrations, for which they were usually paid a small salary. Some performers brought along children as well. Those old enough to shoot or ride often did so in crowd scenes or specialty acts.

Housing

Housing Wild West actors and crew was complicated. Married couples and families had to be kept together. Different ethnic into stacks of three. Conditions were so tight that many chose to sleep on the floor of the equipment cars instead. Sleeping assignments, once made, did not often change.

Once at the grounds of the show, however, the situation was different. Unless the grounds were right up against the railroad, performers moved into tents. Some tents were large, others small. Cody's show generally used tents that were about twelve feet by twelve feet, with enough room inside for two performers and their baggage. Other shows sometimes used larger tents that accommodated more people at once. On occasion Indians, in particular, used tepees rather than canvas tents. Luther Standing Bear remembered what it was like on his trip to Europe:

When the wagon carrying our tipis arrived, some of the boys would roll their blankets around their waists and help unload the wagon. Each man knew his own tipi, and as fast as they were unloaded we would set them up. It was hard work, especially in wet and muddy weather. Bales of straw would be distributed about to put on the ground inside the tipis to keep us out of the mud. In the center of the tipi would be a space for the fire, and after this was started it would not be long before the inside of the tipi would be nice and dry.[107]

groups usually requested that they be given living space of their own. Single women presented even greater problems: it was deemed necessary to keep them well away from any men at night.

The usual system of housing employees included a combination of Pullman sleeping cars and tents. When traveling from one town to another late at night, performers generally slept in double-decker bunks on railroad cars. When possible, actors with similar backgrounds would be paired together: two Cossacks, two cowboys, two sharpshooters. Crew members, on the other hand, were crammed

Not every Wild West performer slept in tents or Pullman cars, of course. On long stands, cast members occasionally stayed in hotels or even in theaters. Annie Oakley remembered trains without sleeping cars, where roustabouts laid down boards each night to turn seats into makeshift beds. Still, most Wild West employees used sleeping cars, tents, or both.

Food

Next to housing their employees, Wild West shows' biggest headache was feeding them. A large show had hundreds of mouths to feed every single day, and Wild West companies had the added problem of being often on the road. Therefore, most touring companies had to carry a cooking tent or a wagon that doubled as a kitchen.

This traveling kitchen was one of the first things to be set up once shows arrived at their next destination. As roustabouts worked and performers unpacked, they grew hungry; while Wild West shows tried to provide good quality food, quickness and efficiency were perhaps more important. "The cook wagons," wrote an observer about the 1925 Miller Brothers' show, "carrying ice boxes with a two-day supply of ice capacity, were marvels of construction. They had been built so that forty minutes after the wagons got on the lot, meals for five hundred persons would be ready." [108] Most kitchens were not quite that efficient, but they all worked toward a similar goal.

Performers and crew received meals as part of their contract. Room and board was typically provided free of charge, although a few promoters hid meal charges in contracts, especially where Indians or other non-English speakers were concerned. The amount of food prepared was staggering. In one week, a newspaper reported, members of Cody's Wild West consumed

Beef 5,694 pounds; veal 1,259 pounds; mutton 750 pounds; pork 966 pounds; bacon 350 pounds; hams 410 pounds; chicken 820 pounds; bread 2,100 loaves; milk 3,260 quarts; ice 10 tons; potatoes 31 barrels; cabbage 7 barrels; spinach 9 barrels; onions 3 barrels; eggs 570 dozen; butter 298 pounds; fish 720 pounds . . . vinegar 6 gallons; catsup 15 gallons; Worcestershire sauce 15 gallons; mustard 6 gallons. . . . [109]

Members of Cody's Wild West show set up camp. Note the combination of tepees and tents.

The list continued for several more lines, including a barrel of pig's feet, four dozen bottles of horseradish, one hundred pounds of salt, ten gallons of syrup, and five hundred pies. Feeding the troupe cost Cody about twenty-five hundred dollars a week.

Cast members ate in communal dining tents. These were large, too: the Miller Brothers' measured 180 feet by 60 feet, or nearly the size of an ice hockey rink. Performers liked the camaraderie that the dining tent provided. Luther Standing Bear recalled about the Sioux who traveled with him to England,

> On rainy days, we always sat inside the big tent. There we could talk about home, home cooking, and the good things we wished we could have to eat that were cooked Indian fashion. Some of the old men would wish for wild peppermint tea and fried bread. Others wished they could have dried meat and bacon, while some wanted roast ribs or choke-cherry soup. We really had plenty to eat, but it was not cooked "Indian style."[110]

Indeed, Cody went out of his way to provide foods that the Indians would like. Although meat was quite expensive in Great Britain, he made sure that the Indians he hired had all of it they wanted.

Dressing Tents

Wild West shows did not all have the same systems for costuming their actors. Some asked cast members to provide clothing that was more or less appropriate for their scenes. Others had seamstresses and tailors on staff to

Providing enough food for the entire cast of a Wild West show was a constant and enormous task. Here, cooks use huge pots to prepare the midday meal.

Performers gather in the mess tent. In one Wild West show, the mess tent was close to the size of a hockey rink.

make costumes. A few of these shows had their performers buy matching outfits directly from the company, and the rest rented or loaned the costumes to the actors. However they were obtained, costumes were vital for every Wild West show, and the dressing tent was therefore important in every performer's daily life.

While star performers like Johnnie Baker had their own private dressing rooms, most cast members were not so lucky. In most shows, performers dressed in one large tent. Men and women sometimes had separate dressing tents, but seem more often to have had separate areas within the same tent. There was little privacy or separation by ethnic group. A Boston newspaper described the dressing tent belonging to Cody's show as follows:

In the center of the tent, whose canvas walls were raised a bit from the ground,

there was a big tub of water, at which everyone drank. At the side were two others, at which everyone so accustomed washed. Around this trunks, boxes, small bits of widely distributed wardrobe, straw, and army accoutrements littered the earth in picturesque disarray. Nearer the outside walls a rope circled the interior of the tent. On this were hung the varied garments of the performers, which formed the semi-screen behind which they dressed.[111]

As for their own personal clothing, most Wild West performers had very little of it. Before the First World War, few people other than the very wealthy owned many changes of clothes. Wild West performers were generally not rich; moreover, many of them led lives in which they were often on the move, in which extra possessions got in the way. Every piece of clothing in a Wild West show had to be transported constantly. Therefore, the limitations on personal belongings were usually strict. Cody constrained his performers to one personal trunk no more than two feet long and eighteen inches high; and he advised cast members, if possible, to dispense with this trunk altogether. As for laundry, Cody required performers to pay a train porter a quarter a week in exchange for bootblacking and laundry services.

Contracts

To join a show, most Wild West performers had to sign a standard contract that governed their behavior and spelled out their responsibilities. Cowboy Harry Webb, who spent time with Cody's Wild West, remembered the contract well. "It had about 50 clauses," he said many years later. "Every one concerned the party of the second part. You promised not to ogle girls, get drunk, swear, or miss a performance. Why, if I got killed, I'd have to pay for my own funeral."[112]

The contracts also covered several other areas of daily life. Gambling was forbidden. So was fighting. Performers had to promise to conduct themselves in an "orderly, quiet, and gentlemanly manner."[113] Not only did performers have to pay for their own funerals, but the companies typically refused to take responsibility for injuries caused by train wrecks or accidents during shows. In fact, shows often helped injured actors anyway, especially if they were hurt while performing. "Once I broke an ankle vaulting onto a galloping horse," remembered Harry Webb. "The colonel [Cody] kept me on the payroll while it healed."[114]

More seriously, contracts told performers what they could and could not do while not performing. Cast members, for instance, were generally not allowed to sit in the grandstand while the show was going on. They were confined to the dressing areas and the offstage section of the arena. Some shows even tried to keep cast and crew members off the main streets of the town and away from local citizens.

There were sound reasons for such policies. Traveling shows had developed bad reputations during the middle part of the nineteenth century—and, in some ways, deservedly so. Carnivals, circuses, and traveling menageries were often legitimate businesses that gave the people of towns they visited good entertainment for their money. Too frequently, however, they promised more than they could deliver, conned townspeople out of their money, and then left for the next town under cover of darkness. Others brought in so-called performers who were mainly interested in starting fights, destroying property, and stealing. Such activities did not qualify as entertainments and did not serve to give show business a good name. Keeping Wild West performers on show grounds was partly a way of reassuring critics of the shows, who worried that their towns would be overrun with hard-drinking, quick-draw cowboys out to stir up trouble.

Of course, not all shows refused to allow their performers to mix with locals. In some circumstances, it would have been impossible. Cast members on tour often had no time to leave the show grounds, but members of shows that stayed in one place did. There were occasional days off, too. Indeed, many cast and crew members enjoyed their time exploring towns and cities. On a trip to England, Luther Standing Bear remembered many Sioux using the time between performances to go shopping in town for trinkets, blankets, and other souvenirs. Other Indians, cowboys, and marksmen mentioned their excitement at seeing sights like Buckingham Palace in England, the World's Fair in Chicago, the Leaning Tower of Pisa, and the oceans in various seaboard cities.

And not all Wild West performers could entirely control themselves, contract or no contract. In 1899, Pawnee Bill's show paraded through the streets of Princeton, New Jersey, where some students at Princeton University got into a fight with Pawnee Bill's horsemen. A potentially more serious situation occurred in Cheyenne, Wyoming, in 1884. According to the local newspaper,

Last night at 12 o'clock, cowboys belonging to Hardwick's Wild West Show made a drunken raid on South Clark street in regular western style. They succeeded in frightening the people from the streets, and were finally captured by the police and locked up. Twelve large navy revolvers and a large knife were secured. The entire party was bailed out this morning, and this afternoon gave the usual exhibition to a crowd of 12,000 people. The cowboys in their raid last night were led by Ben Circkle, for years a celebrated character in the far West.[115]

Despite the lighthearted tone of the article, Wild West promoters who read it could not have been pleased by the behavior of Circkle and his friends.

A Virtual City

Cast members of larger shows, however, were able to live quite comfortably without ever going off the show grounds. A show like

---

"He Has Tried to Scalp His Sister"

Children who watched Wild West shows often tried to imitate them at home. Sometimes this took on the form of attempting to get the family dog to buck, or staging a mock battle with forefingers standing in for guns. "On occasion," wrote Don Russell in *The Wild West*, "the town's children would pool their talents, pony carts, bicycles, band instruments, and borrowed finery and put on a show of their own." Sometimes, though, children caused injuries to each other after watching a show. At least one boy shot another while trying to imitate a trick of Annie Oakley's. Another child died after being burned at the stake. The following poem, quoted in Sarah Blackstone's *Buckskin, Business, and Bullets*, was a humorous way of dealing with the situation:

A Youthful Terror

He has tried to scalp his sister,
He's lassoed the Thomas cat,
He has shot my English setter,
And tomahawked my hat.

He has frightened his poor mother
Into forty-seven fits,
He has broken all the ornaments
Into fifty-seven bits.

Oh! how I rue the day
That I was made to go
And take my son and heir to see
That wild and Western show.

Cody's, Pawnee Bill's, or the 101 Ranch provided most necessities on site. Not only did the shows take charge of feeding and housing performers, but shows carried other specialists as well: barbers to cut cast members' hair, gunsmiths and blacksmiths to make and repair equipment, shoemakers to produce a new pair of shoes when necessary. Performers also could attend Sunday morning religious services without leaving the grounds. In Cody's show these services were courtesy of cast member Jim Mitchell, known as the Cowboy Preacher. A story about him claims that several buffalo escaped from their corral once while he was preaching. He grabbed a pony, excused himself for a moment, and herded them back where they belonged before finishing the sermon.

And it was not hard to find entertainment right on the premises, either. Many performers sang to pass the hours or while working: cowboy songs for the cowboys, traditional music for the Native Americans. Though there was not much formal rehearsing during the tours, performers often discussed their work, taught each other new skills, and sometimes showed off tricks they were learning. This was especially common on long voyages, such as those across the Atlantic. On one trip, Annie Oakley is said to have lassoed two ship officers in a doorway. People who could tell jokes or tall stories were much in demand, and those who were skilled in crafts like whittling often used their time that way.

Then there were games. Adults played cards, often for money, and board games like checkers. Children played, too. Some set up swings on any available branch or cable. One commentator mentioned "juvenile antics" on the ground, "such as the wild shouting accompanying 'Run Sheep Run,' or the squeals and screams of a game of 'tag.'" [116] Other chil-

In their off hours, Native Americans play ping pong on a makeshift table. Such respite was infrequent as cast members often had to perform in up to three shows per day.

Accidents on Parade

Train wrecks and horse spills were not the only cause of injury in Wild West shows. Twice in 1896 Cody's show suffered serious accidents—during a morning parade. In August, bandwagon driver Edward Fletcher was killed when the reins slipped out of his hand. He bent over to pick them up, lost his balance, hit the pavement with his head, and fractured his skull.

An even more bizarre accident had seriously injured six band members a month earlier during a parade in Massilon, Ohio. According to the 1896 route book, as quoted in Michael Masterson's *Sounds of the Frontier: Music in Buffalo Bill's Wild West*, a bandwagon attempted to go under a bridge without sufficient clearance.

"The driver of the eight-horse bandwagon did not notice that the bridge was low. . . . The leaders of the team were under the bridge before the driver noticed that it was too low, but then it was too late for him to check [halt] his team. The heavy steel structure scraped the men from their seats like ten-pins. Screams and cries from the wounded men rent the air, and the wagon appeared on the opposite side of the bridge before the team came to a halt."

Masterson conjectures that the men were too busy playing their instruments to see the bridge. Apparently none of them was killed, but most were badly injured, one so seriously he was not at first expected to live.

dren's games were less organized. The Indian children of the 101 Ranch Wild West, said one observer,

ran, played, shouted, and effervesced with life and spirits, like children the world over. The older boys were armed with bows and headless arrows, and practiced shooting continually—at a mark or for distance, or vertically into the air. . . . Many of the young braves engaged in sham battles, conducting a mimic fight much after the manner of men, except that they used mud balls. The little girls made dolls and other toys of buckskin, and built playhouses like their white sisters.[117]

But life in a Wild West show was not all fun and games by any means. The work was hard and often monotonous. A schedule that included a parade in the morning, a performance in the afternoon, another performance in the evening, and travel by train during the night wore cast members down. Even those who liked new people and places often found the travel wearying. Many performers found themselves longing for home well before the show closed each fall. Only a few cast members returned year after year. Annie Oakley was one. When she and her husband had a house built, they realized they were so used to touring that they had forgotten to put in any closets.

"It's Hell"

And sometimes Wild West life did worse than make people homesick. There were the train crashes, of course, and the injuries during performances. There were also illnesses. Indians, not having all the immunities of the white performers, were especially likely to die of diseases they contracted. During a flu epidemic in Spain, several members of Cody's

In this incongruous scene, Bill Cody and members of the Wild West show tour Venice in a gondola.

show died. Announcer Frank Richmond was one, and two or three white roustabouts also were killed by the virus, but the bulk of the dead were Indians. Some shows gave smallpox vaccinations to all their employees. Unfortunately, these were painful. They often made performers' arms so sore they could barely lift a gun or hold the reins of a horse, let alone stay on a bucking bronco or shoot glass balls thrown randomly into the air.

But the worst part of Wild West show life may have been the weather. Though the grandstands were covered, the arenas typically were not. Promoters had expenses whether the show went on or not. Any ticket sold was money toward recovering those costs. Thus, Wild West shows were rarely canceled due to weather. If the attendance was nine or nine thousand, the show went on. Performers and crew members alike remembered miserable weather years after they had left Wild West shows. Some left their shows because of it. After a series of rainy days, sharpshooter Adam Bogardus pulled out of

Cody's show; he could no longer take the constant wet, chilly weather. Others just put up with it. Said one cowboy,

> A Wild West show in bad weather, it's hell, and when the weather is good, why it's beautiful. So we have good, bad, and indifferent. And then plain hell. Because when it's raining and snowing and the lot is all nothing but mud, why you're riding a buckin' horse there or anything, and you happen to fall in the mud and roll around, why by the time you got to the back end you wouldn't know your outfit.[118]

Bad weather, train travel, card games, songs, and cafeteria-style food—all were part of the daily life of Wild West performers. Cast and crew members both had to find ways of dealing with all the aspects of life in the Wild West, both good and bad. Those who could not either left the show or were miserable. But those who did usually ended up with a rewarding experience as Wild West personnel.

The Death of the Wild West

In 1914, the First World War began. Although the United States would not be directly involved for three years, the war nevertheless had a huge effect on traveling Wild West shows. Many companies were trapped in Europe and had difficulty escaping. Some Cossacks and other European actors returned to their home nations and never came back. Zack Miller's 101 Ranch show lost most of its livestock to the war effort, too; except for a few highly trained and prized horses, the English government took the company's animals, paying Miller a small fee, and put them to work for the country. Thus, some of the outfits that had been touring Europe came back much smaller and somewhat poorer than they had been when they had left.

The war played a bigger role than that, however. Shows had been increasingly counting on the European market. By some estimates, as many as fifty Wild West shows, most of them very small, had been touring England and the European continent when war was declared. There was neither room nor business enough for all of them at home. Many, perhaps most, went out of business and never reopened.

In 1917, the United States joined the war. Some performers signed up to fight, leading more Wild West shows to fold. There were

Some companies of traveling Wild West shows were trapped in Europe once World War I began.

Horsemen perform in the Wild West show. The shows declined after World War I for a number of reasons but primarily because people found them antiquated and dull.

restrictions on travel and electricity, which also hurt, and there were fewer people spending less money on the home front. Entertainments like Wild West shows seemed more like a luxury than a necessity.

Still, when the war was over, Wild West shows did not return to normal. Their era was more or less done. Occasional shows, even large ones, still played, such as the 101 Ranch show that toured for several years in the 1920s. But the period of greatest popularity was over.

In part, this was due to changes in society. As the economy boomed during the 1920s, it became harder for Wild West shows to pay competitive salaries. Even cowboys—of whom there were fewer and fewer—had job offers that paid better than the remaining Wild West shows could match. Entertain-

ment tastes were also an issue. By 1920, movies were drawing the crowds. Sports, too, were blossoming. The Wild West show had a hard time competing. Even the automobile's sudden popularity played a part: with city streets full of cars, parades became harder and harder to route through downtowns and finally stopped altogether.

But perhaps the biggest problem Wild West shows faced was that they seemed dated, old-fashioned, even dull. By 1920 or so the West was no longer "wild," and had not been wild for at least three decades. With each succeeding year, it became harder to pass off the show as current. Indians had been defeated, cowboys were out of the popular mind: the Wild West was a thing of the past. Indeed, even by the turn of the century, Cody's show was having trouble with relevance. One newspaper reporter wrote in 1900,

> The attacks on the emigrant train, the settler's cabin and the Deadwood coach and the buffalo hunt are a bit perfunctory in their nature now, because they no longer represent things which are. The military features have risen into greater prominence because they illustrate the things that are now in everybody's mind.[119]

If newspapers could complain about the show being out of date in 1900, it was clearly all the more so twenty years later.

History Lives On

But Wild West shows do live today, in several different forms. There are a few companies that re-create shows like Cody's. Pawnee, Oklahoma, sponsors a reenactment of Pawnee Bill's Wild West each summer, using all-volunteer casts. "The show is rip-roaring, rough-riding, shoot-em-up, down-home, family-fun entertainment," says one participant.[120] Nor are they limited to traditional Western areas. In the summer of 1997, for example, one out-fit performed regularly at an arena in Naperville, Illinois.

Rodeos still exist, including professional circuits with standardized events, prize money, and rules. Wild West clubs flourish, too, not only in America but also in places such as Germany, where the study of the Wild West is especially popular. And finally, Western movies are similar in some very important ways to the Wild West shows of the past. But Wild West shows as Cody, Lillie, Oakley, Miller, and the rest knew them are gone forever.

Still, the importance of these shows cannot be dismissed. They had value beyond mere entertainment. They helped create the image Americans have today of the West, an image that is accurate in many ways, if flawed in others. They exposed thousands of people to cowboys, cowgirls, sharpshooters, and most particularly Indians. They broadened the horizons of hundreds upon hundreds of cast and crew members who got to see places they had barely heard of and people they never knew existed; they also established an unusually diverse workplace and community for the time. And throughout, they stirred up hopes and dreams and excitement for many, many audiences. The men and women who traveled with Wild West shows live on today as participants in an important slice of American history.

Notes

Chapter 1: The Origins of the Wild West

1. Quoted in Don Russell, *The Wild West*. Fort Worth, TX: Amon Carter Museum of Western Art, 1970, p. 2.
2. Quoted in Joseph G. Rosa and Robin May, *Buffalo Bill and His Wild West*. Lawrence: University of Kansas Press, 1989, p. 66.
3. Sarah Blackstone, *Buckskins, Bullets, and Business: A History of Buffalo Bill's Wild West*. Westport, CT: Greenwood Press, 1986, p. 7.
4. William F. Cody, *Story of the Wild West and Camp-Fire Chats*. Freeport, NY: Books for Libraries Press, 1970 reprint, p. 648.
5. Cody, *Story of the Wild West*, p. 651.
6. Don Russell, *The Lives and Legends of Buffalo Bill*. Norman: University of Oklahoma Press, 1960, pp. 194–95.
7. Cody, *Story of the Wild West*, p. 651.
8. Quoted in Russell, *Lives and Legends*, p. 198.
9. Quoted in Russell, *Lives and Legends*, p. 263.
10. Quoted in Russell, *Lives and Legends*, p. 286.
11. Cody, *Story of the Wild West*, p. 689.
12. Quoted in Blackstone, *Buckskins, Bullets, and Business*, p. 12.
13. Quoted in Russell, *Lives and Legends*, p. 291.
14. Quoted in Russell, *Lives and Legends*, p. 289.
15. Cody, *Story of the Wild West*, p. 693.
16. Quoted in Russell, *Lives and Legends*, p. 294.
17. Quoted in Russell, *Lives and Legends*, p. 299.

Chapter 2: The Shows

18. Russell, *The Wild West*, p. 68.
19. R. L. Heminger, "Annie Oakley Plinked 'em All," *The Courier* (Findlay, OH), http://www.thecourier.com/opinion/Historic/r1031596.htm.
20. Quoted in Michael Masterson, "Sounds of the Frontier: Music in Buffalo Bill's Wild West" (Ph.D. diss. University of New Mexico, 1990), p. 304.
21. Quoted in Dee Brown, *The American West*. New York: Scribner's, 1994, pp. 381–82.
22. Quoted in Russell, *The Wild West*, p. 74.
23. Quoted in Masterson, "Sounds of the Frontier," p. 304.
24. Quoted in Rosa and May, *Buffalo Bill*, p. 132.
25. Quoted in Rosa and May, *Buffalo Bill*, p. 166.
26. Quoted in Blackstone, *Buckskins, Bullets, and Business*, p. 56.
27. Quoted in Masterson, "Sounds of the Frontier," p. 304.
28. Quoted in Rosa and May, *Buffalo Bill*, p. 88.
29. Quoted in Rosa and May, *Buffalo Bill*, pp. 88-89.
30. Ellsworth Collings, in collaboration with Alma Miller England, *The 101 Ranch*.

Norman: University of Oklahoma Press, 1937, p. 163.

31. Quoted in Glenn Shirley, *Pawnee Bill*. Lincoln: University of Nebraska Press, 1958, p. 168.

32. Quoted in Shirley, *Pawnee Bill*, p. 169.

33. Quoted in Blackstone, *Buckskins, Bullets, and Business*, p. 55.

34. Quoted in Blackstone, *Buckskins, Bullets, and Business*, p. 31.

35. Quoted in Blackstone, *Buckskins, Bullets, and Business*, pp. 62–63.

36. Quoted in Rosa and May, *Buffalo Bill*, p. 167.

37. Collings, *The 101 Ranch*, p. 183.

Chapter 3: The Performers

38. Collings, *The 101 Ranch*, p. 162.

39. Collings, *The 101 Ranch*, p. 165.

40. Quoted in Russell, *Lives and Legends*, p. 306.

41. Quoted in Russell, *Lives and Legends*, p. 305.

42. Quoted in Collings, *The 101 Ranch*, p. 171.

43. Clifford Westermeier, *Trailing the Cowboy*. Caldwell, ID: Caxton Press, 1955, p. 86.

44. Mary Lou LeCompte, *Cowgirls of the Rodeo: Pioneer Professional Athletes*. Urbana: University of Illinois Press, 1993, p. 3.

45. Quoted in Russell, *The Wild West*, p. 79.

46. Collings, *The 101 Ranch*, p. 180.

47. Quoted in Russell, *Lives and Legends*, p. 311.

48. Quoted in Masterson, "Sounds of the Frontier," p. 304.

49. Courtney Ryley Cooper, *Annie Oakley: Woman at Arms*. London: Hurst and Blackett, 1927, p. 111.

50. *Buffalo Bill's Wild West and Congress of Rough Riders of the World*, Chicago: Blakely Printing, 1893, p. 54.

51. Quoted in Blackstone, *Buckskins, Bullets, and Business*, p. 65.

Chapter 4: Native Americans

52. Quoted in Russell, *The Wild West*, p. 67.

53. Quoted in L. C. Moses, *Wild West Shows and the Images of the American Indians, 1883–1933*. Albuquerque: University of New Mexico Press, 1996, p. 27.

54. Quoted in Moses, *Wild West Shows*, p. 27.

55. Quoted in Moses, *Wild West Shows*, p. 75.

56. Quoted in Russell, *The Wild West*, p. 64.

57. Quoted in Blackstone, *Buckskins, Bullets, and Business*, p. 86.

58. Quoted in Moses, *Wild West Shows*, p. 103.

59. Quoted in Moses, *Wild West Shows*, p. 103.

60. John G. Neihardt, *Black Elk Speaks*. New York: Pocket Books, 1972, p. 183.

61. Quoted in Moses, *Wild West Shows*, p. 64.

62. Quoted in Rosa and May, *Buffalo Bill*, p. 140.

63. Quoted in Moses, *Wild West Shows*, p. 30.

64. Collings, *The 101 Ranch*, p. 185.

65. Luther Standing Bear, *My People the Sioux*. New York: Houghton Mifflin, 1928, p. 252.

66. Collings, *The 101 Ranch*, p. 170.
67. Standing Bear, *My People the Sioux*, p. 266.
68. Quoted in Moses, *Wild West Shows*, p. 180.
69. Quoted in Russell, *Lives and Legends*, p. 316.
70. Isabelle S. Sayers, *Annie Oakley and Buffalo Bill's Wild West*. New York: Dover Publications, 1981, p. 22.
71. Quoted in Russell, *The Wild West*, p. 24.
72. Quoted in Moses, *Wild West Shows*, p. 117.
73. Neihardt, *Black Elk Speaks*, p. 186.
74. Neihardt, *Black Elk Speaks*, p. 187.
75. Neihardt, *Black Elk Speaks*, p. 194.
76. Quoted in Rosa and May, *Buffalo Bill*, p. 91.
77. Quoted in Dee Brown, *The Westerners*. New York: Holt, Rinehart and Winston, 1974, p. 255.
78. Quoted in Moses, *Wild West Shows*, p. 44.
79. Quoted in Moses, *Wild West Shows*, p. 75.
80. Quoted in Moses, *Wild West Shows*, p. 76.
81. Quoted in Moses, *Wild West Shows*, p. 66.
82. Quoted in Moses, *Wild West Shows*, p. 175.
83. Standing Bear, *My People the Sioux*, p. 263.
84. Standing Bear, *My People the Sioux*, p. 261.
85. *Buffalo Bill's Wild West and Congress of Rough Riders of the World*, p. 34.
86. Quoted in Moses, *Wild West Shows*, p. 200.
87. Quoted in Alice J. Hall, "Buffalo Bill and the Enduring West," *National Geographic*, July 1981, p. 84.

Chapter 5: On the Move

88. R. L. Heminger, "When Buffalo Bill Came to Town," *The Courier* (Findlay, Ohio), http://www.thecourier.com/opinion/Historic/r1030896.htm.
89. Quoted in Russell, *Lives and Legends*, p. 443.
90. Cooper, *Annie Oakley: Woman at Arms*, p. 190.
91. Quoted in Blackstone, *Buckskins, Bullets, and Business*, p. 50.
92. Collings, *The 101 Ranch*, pp. 186–87.
93. Cooper, *Annie Oakley: Woman at Arms*, p. 96.
94. Heminger, "When Buffalo Bill Came to Town."
95. Blackstone, *Buckskins, Bullets, and Business*, p. 45.
96. Blackstone, *Buckskins, Bullets, and Business*, p. 40.
97. Cooper, *Annie Oakley: Woman at Arms*, p. 20.
98. Cooper, *Annie Oakley: Woman at Arms*, p. 114.
99. Quoted in Blackstone, *Buckskins, Bullets, and Business*, p. 22.
100. Quoted in Russell, *The Wild West*, p. 19.
101. Quoted in Russell, *The Wild West*, p. 19.
102. Quoted in Russell, *Lives and Legends*, p. 327.
103. Standing Bear, *My People the Sioux*, p. 271.

Chapter 6: Daily Life

104. Quoted in Blackstone, *Buckskins, Bullets, and Business*, p. 77.
105. Quoted in Shirley, *Pawnee Bill*, p. 195.

106. Quoted in Shirley, *Pawnee Bill*, p. 195.

107. Standing Bear, *My People the Sioux*, pp. 259–60.

108. Collings, *The 101 Ranch*, p. 184.

109. Quoted in Blackstone, *Buckskins, Bullets, and Business*, p. 47.

110. Standing Bear, *My People the Sioux*, p. 263.

111. Quoted in Blackstone, *Buckskins, Bullets, and Business*, p. 41.

112. Quoted in Hall, "Buffalo Bill and the Enduring West," p. 81.

113. Quoted in Blackstone, *Buckskins, Bullets, and Business*, p. 79.

114. Quoted in Hall, "Buffalo Bill and the Enduring West," p. 81.

115. Quoted in Brown, *The American West*, p. 379.

116. Cooper, *Annie Oakley: Woman at Arms*, p. 107.

117. Collings, *The 101 Ranch*, pp. 169–70.

118. Quoted in Blackstone, *Buckskins, Bullets, and Business*, p. 35.

Epilogue: The Death of the Wild West

119. *New-York Daily Tribune*, "The Rough Riders Return," April 24, 1900, p. 7.

120. Donald Stotts, "Pawnee Bill Wild West Show Puts Excitement in Economic Development," http://www.okstate.edu/OSU_Ag/agedcm4h/ag_news/0617paw.txt.

For Further Reading

Alice J. Hall, "Buffalo Bill and the Enduring West," *National Geographic*, July 1981. A short article with a focus on Cody's contributions to making the West what it was. Includes some information on Wild West shows and interviews with people who had connections with Cody's troupe.

Walter Havighurst, *Buffalo Bill's Great Wild West Show*. New York: Random House, 1957. An outline of the history of Cody's show, from the beginning to the end, with special emphasis on some of the acts. Intended for children and young adults.

Ellen Levine, *Ready, Aim, Fire!: The Real Adventures of Annie Oakley*. New York: Scholastic, 1989. A short but thorough biography of Oakley, giving plenty of information about her role in Wild West shows and her feelings about what she did there.

John G. Neihardt, *Black Elk Speaks*. New York: Pocket Books, 1972. Neihardt took down the words of the Sioux spiritual leader Black Elk. Most of the book is given over to Black Elk's thoughts about religion and the disasters that befell the Sioux, but there is one chapter on Black Elk's experience touring Europe with a Wild West show.

Joseph G. Rosa and Robin May, *Buffalo Bill and His Wild West*. Lawrence: University of Kansas Press, 1989. An especially well-illustrated book covering all parts of Cody's show, with an emphasis on Cody himself. Many wonderful photographs and reproductions of documents.

Don Russell, *The Wild West*. Fort Worth, TX: Amon Carter Museum of Western Art, 1970. Another impressive book for pictures, many in full color. Especially notable for the reproductions of advertising posters from various shows. This book tells about shows in general, unlike most others, which focus more on Cody's; still, Cody's show is the one that crops up most, even here.

William R. Sanford and Carl R. Green, *Buffalo Bill Cody: Showman of the Wild West*. Springfield, NJ: Enslow Publishing, 1996. Another book aimed primarily at children and young adults, this one focuses on Cody, especially in his role as founder of Wild West shows.

Clifford Westermeier, *Trailing the Cowboy*. Caldwell, ID: Caxton Press, 1955. A description of cowboy life; useful for understanding the background of many performers and the origin of some of the acts.

Works Consulted

Sarah Blackstone, *Buckskins, Bullets, and Business: A History of Buffalo Bill's Wild West*. Westport, CT: Greenwood Press, 1986. An excellent, thoroughly researched book covering almost all aspects of Cody's show, with reference to other shows where helpful. Especially helpful for origins and logistics.

Dee Brown, *The American West*. New York: Scribner's, 1994. Good background reading about the West and its history; some brief information about the shows, but more interested in rodeo.

————, *Bury My Heart at Wounded Knee: An Indian History of the American West*. New York: Holt, Rinehart and Winston, 1970. The history of the Indian wars in the second half of the nineteenth century. Essential for understanding the period and the role of the Indians in shows.

————, *The Westerners*. New York: Holt, Rinehart and Winston, 1974. More good background reading about the people who settled the West and how the region has changed in the last two centuries.

Buffalo Bill's Wild West and Congress of Rough Riders of the World. Chicago: Blakely Printing Co., 1893. The program from Cody's 1893 season in Chicago. A wonderful storehouse of information regarding acts, origins, and personalities. Well illustrated.

William F. Cody, *Story of the Wild West and Camp-Fire Chats*. Freeport, NY: Books for Libraries Press, 1970 reprint. An autobiography—one of many that Cody wrote. Especially strong on the origins of the Wild West show. Cody describes how and why the Wild West came to be and tells in detail abut his first trip to Europe. Some of the details should not be taken as completely accurate.

Ellsworth Collings, in collaboration with Alma Miller England, *The 101 Ranch*. Norman: University of Oklahoma Press, 1937. A history of the 101 Ranch, with some mention of its Wild West show. Some information about rodeo and other similar entertainments as well.

Courtney Ryley Cooper, *Annie Oakley: Woman at Arms*. London: Hurst and Blackett, 1927. A biography of Annie Oakley, written by a man who knew her personally. Though the book sometimes makes up dialogue, it is a useful source for Oakley's early life as well as for her time touring with Cody's show.

Dexter W. Fellowes and Andrew A. Freeman, *This Way to the Big Show*. New York: Halcyon House, 1938. Fellowes was a press agent for Cody's show; the book covers show business in general at the time and Fellowes's life in it.

Carolyn Thomas Forman, *Indians Abroad*. Norman: University of Oklahoma Press, 1943. A scholarly work about Indians who traveled to other countries. The book begins in the very early days of European settlement and continues through the Depression. One or two chapters deal with Wild West shows and the Indians who traveled with them.

Neil Harris, *Humbug: The Art of P. T. Barnum*. Chicago: University of Chicago Press, 1973. A fine biography of Barnum. Helpful in giving a sense of show business at the time, as well as citing Barnum's own "Wild West" attempts.

Justin Haywood, "Go West, Young Man," *Chicago Reader*, August 15, 1997. A description of the revival Wild West show in Naperville, Illinois, during the summer of 1997. Some historical background as well.

R. L. Heminger, "Annie Oakley Plinked 'em All," *The Courier* (Findlay, OH), http://www.thecourier.com/opinion/Historic/r1031596.htm. These articles are reminiscences of Wild West shows by people who attended them as children. Short but useful.

———, "When Buffalo Bill Came to Town," *The Courier* (Findlay, OH), http://www.thecourier.com/opinion/Historic/r1030896.htm.

Elizabeth Atwood Lawrence, *Rodeo*. Knoxville: The University of Tennessee Press, 1982. A thorough history of rodeo in all its forms. Some information on Wild West performers and the connection between rodeo and the Wild West.

Mary Lou LeCompte, *Cowgirls of the Rodeo: Pioneer Professional Athletes*. Urbana: University of Illinois Press, 1993. Another book that focuses primarily on rodeo, only this one limits its focus to the women who participated. Many of them were Wild West performers, too, and the book does a good job of covering that part of their careers. Interesting and informative.

Michael Masterson, "Sounds of the Frontier: Music in Buffalo Bill's Wild West" (Ph.D. diss., University of New Mexico, 1990). A very detailed look at the lives of the bandsmen in Cody's Wild West—what they played, how they were hired, what their responsibilities were.

L. C. Moses, *Wild West Shows and the Images of the American Indians, 1883–1933*. Albuquerque: University of New Mexico Press, 1996. The definitive work on Indians in Wild West shows. Tremendously thorough and full of wonderful quotations. Moses' perspective in that Wild West shows were not as bad for Indians as is commonly believed.

John Young Nelson, *Fifty Years on the Trail: A True Story of Western Life*. Norman: University of Oklahoma Press, 1963. Nelson performed with Cody. This autobiography does not cover the Wild West years, but it does give good background on the life of at least one featured performer.

New-York Daily Tribune, "The Rough Riders Return," April 24, 1900. A review of Cody's show appearing in New York City.

Don Russell, *The Lives and Legends of Buffalo Bill*. Norman: University of Oklahoma Press, 1960. The definitive biography of Cody, though there are many competitors. Written in an appealing, humorous style and extremely informative; several chapters relate to the Wild West shows.

Isabelle S. Sayers, *Annie Oakley and Buffalo Bill's Wild West*. New York: Dover Publications, 1981. A well-illustrated book exploring the connection between Cody and Oakley. The author gives much good background information.

Glenn Shirley, *Pawnee Bill*. Lincoln: University of Nebraska Press, 1958. A biography of Gordon Lillie, also known as Pawnee

Bill. A few chapters mention his Wild West show.

Spokane Spokesman-Review, "Long Trip Home." September 29, 1997. A newspaper article dealing with the reburial of Long Wolf and White Star.

Luther Standing Bear, *My People the Sioux*. New York: Houghton Mifflin, 1928. A fascinating autobiography. The end of the book tells much about Cody's show going to Britain. Standing Bear was part of both the white world and the Indian one; his feelings of being pulled both ways are very clear in his descriptions of life in the show.

Donald Stotts, "Pawnee Bill Wild West Show Puts Excitement in Economic Development," http://www.okstate.edu/OSU_Ag/agedcm4h/ag_news/0617pawn.txt. A description of the revival Wild West show in Pawnee, Oklahoma.

Raymond Thorpe, *Spirit Gun of the West: The Story of Doc W. F. Carver*. Glendale, CA: A. H. Clark, 1957. A not-always-reliable account of a not-always-reliable man and his life, with some description of the Carver-Cody partnership and the first Wild West show.

Time-Life Books, *The Wild West*. New York: Warner Books, 1993. A well-illustrated historical account of the West in the nineteenth century. Good background information, and a small amount of detail on Wild West shows.

George E. Virgines, "101 Wild West Show Posters," *Antiques and Collecting Hobbies*, July, 1990. A short article explaining the why and the how of Wild West advertising. Illustrated with examples of posters used by the 101 Wild West show.

Index

Picture Credits

Cover photo: Peter Newark's Western Americana
Archive Photos, 46, 50, 55, 75
John Burke/Stock Montage, 66
Corbis-Bettmann, 9, 14, 17, 18, 20 (Right), 29, 40, 59
Denver Public Library/ Western History Department, 15, 20 (Left), 22, 24, 25, 27(both), 28, 30, 33, 34, 35, 37, 41, 42, 44, 51, 52, 58, 60, 61, 64, 65, 73, 74, 78, 80, 82
Library of Congress 11, 13 (both), 48
National Archives, 81
Stock Montage, Inc., 31, 39
Woodfin Camp and Associates, Inc./Wyoming State Museum, 8

About the Author

Stephen Currie is the author of more than twenty books and many magazine articles. Among his nonfiction titles are *Music in the Civil War, Birthday a Day, Problem Play,* and *We Have Marched Together: The Working Children's Crusade*. He is also a first and second grade teacher. He grew up in Chicago, where he spent many hours laboriously composing stories on an ancient manual typewriter, and now lives in Poughkeepsie, New York, with his wife, Amity, and two children, Irene and Nicholas.